CRITIQUE OF PRACTICAL REASON

Jmmanuel Kant geb. den 22sten April 1724
wohnte bei Buchh... u Kanter von 1766 bis 1769
ward für dessen Laden gemalt im August 1768
vom Portraitmaler Becker starb 1804 den 12ten Februar.

CRITIQUE OF PRACTICAL REASON

and other Works on the Theory of Ethics

Immanuel Kant

Translated by Thomas Kingsmill Abbott

Introduction by Dennis Sweet, Ph.D.

BARNES
& NOBLE
BOOKS
NEW YORK

CONTENTS

PART SECOND

METHODOLOGY OF PURE PRACTICAL REASON

INTRODUCTION

CRITIQUE *of Practical Reason* was the second of Immanuel Kant's three 'critiques,' the three pillars of his Critical philosophy. It was also the second of his three mature writings in ethics. In both contexts, the book has suffered the fate of many a middle child and has often been overshadowed by its siblings. This is partly due to the style and the structure of the book. Even at his best, Kant, as a writer, is extremely demanding of his reader. The book also presupposes a familiarity with his previous philosophical innovations; specifically, with the 'transcendental' procedure introduced in the *Critique of Pure Reason*, whereby one starts from some ordinary experience and deduces the necessary conditions for such an experience. Furthermore, it assumes a familiarity with his earlier work on moral philosophy, the *Foundations of the Metaphysics of Morals*. It is no surprise, then, that the *Critique of Practical Reason* has remained terra incognita among many of his readers. The book does, however, fulfill a critical purpose in Kant's Critical philosophy by reinstating the notions of human freedom, God, and the immortal soul into philosophical discourse; notions which, in the first Critique, had been shown to be unsuitable in their traditional applications in the realm of metaphysics. In the *Critique of Practical Reason*, these ideas are given a home; they are ideas of pure practical reason, or transcendental conditions of our moral activity. Thus, the second Critique is the fulfillment of Kant's important promise in the first Critique, "to deny knowledge, in order to make room for faith."

No philosopher has exerted more influence on modern philosophy than Immanuel Kant. He was born on April 22, 1724, in Königsberg, East Prussia. During his lifetime the intellectual milieu in Germany was divided into two radically opposed camps. On the one hand, there were the pietists, followers of a religious movement that began at the end of the sixteenth century, which stood in stark contrast to the attitudes that formed the *Aufklärung*, or the German Enlightenment. On the other hand, there were the views of the 'dogmatic' rationalist philosophers, G. W. Leibniz (1646-1716) and his student and popularizer, Christian Wolff (1679-1754). While pietism stressed personal freedom and the subjective aspects of faith as the most important elements of human reality, the dogmatists emphasized the priority of reason and objectivity in human concerns. Although Kant was raised as a pietist, he was for the most part educated in the rationalist tradition. And much of his genius consists in his ability to create a new alternative, a synthesis of these two seemingly disparate strands. Nowhere is this more evident than in the *Critique of Practical Reason*, where, employing the objectively rational methods of his new transcendental philosophy, he attempts to secure what had traditionally been regarded as the purely subjective components of moral motivation, i.e., the beliefs in God and the immortal soul.

Prior to 1781, during his so-called pre-Critical period, Kant wrote nearly two-dozen treatises and essays on a broad range of topics in philosophy, physics, natural history, geology, and theology. It is, however, 1781 that truly marks the beginning of his most productive period. It was this year that he published the *Kritik der reinen Vernunft*, the *Critique of Pure Reason*, arguably the most important and original contribution to modern philosophy. This was followed two years later by the *Prolegomena zu einer jeden künftigen Metaphysik, die als Wissenschaft wird auftreten können (Prolegomena for a Future Metaphysics That Can Appear as a Science)*, which is essentially a summation and restatement of the arguments in the first Critique. Among the more important works that followed were the *Grundlegung zur Metaphysik der Sitten (Foundations of the Metaphysics of Morals*), certainly the most accessible of Kant's books and one of the most important contributions in moral philosophy ever written. In 1788, Kant published his second Critique, the *Kritik der practischen Vernunft*, the *Critique of Practical Reason*. This was followed in 1790 by the third and final Critique, the *Kritik der Urtheilskraft*, the *Critique of Judgment*, which is his transcendental exposition of teleological and aesthetic judgments. In 1793 Kant published *Religion innerhalb der Grenzen der blossen Vernunft* (*Religion Within the Bounds of Reason Alone*), which earned him a royal censure. And in 1797, Kant published his final work on ethics, *Die Metaphysik der Sitten* (*The Metaphysics of Morals*). He died in 1804.

The significance of the *Critique of Practical Reason* can only be understood when it is placed in the context of Kant's other works; specifically, the first Critique and the *Foundations*. In the *Critique of Pure Reason*, Kant had attempted to show the failure of previous attempts to establish metaphysical claims beyond the domain of human knowledge, and to answer the question, how are a priori synthetic judgments possible? In the former context, traditional metaphysics and 'rational theology' had attempted to prove the existence of God, the immortal soul, and human freedom by the use of discursive reason. Kant contends that such arguments are, however, misguided attempts to employ reason beyond its proper domain. In criticizing the traditional dogmatic arguments for God and the soul, he earned for himself the title *Alleszerstörer*, the "all destroyer." In the latter context, Kant attempts to establish the truths of mathematics and metaphysics as a priori, i.e., necessary and universally true assertions, and as synthetic judgments, i.e., judgments about experience.

The issues Kant deals with in the *Critique of Pure Reason* have to do more or less exclusively with the domain of *theoretical reason*; the realm of human knowledge wherein truth can be verified through empirical procedures. The concerns that had traditionally been the subject matter of metaphysics, e.g., the existence of God, the immortal soul, and human freedom, inasmuch as they are unverifiable by empirical means, are, for Kant, excluded from the domain of metaphysics. They are outside the limits of theoretical reason. Yet, they fall within the purview of what Kant calls *practical reason.* Practical reason has to do with issues that have pragmatic significance for human beings, but which, alas, cannot be known by us in any normal manner. For Kant, questions of faith and morality are issues of practical reason.

Kant's first detailed attempt to deal with the practical application of reason to moral issues occurs in his little work entitled the *Foundations of the Metaphysics of Morals.* Here he begins by examining various common kinds of moral judgments and concludes that inasmuch as such judgments are *hypothetical,* i.e., to the extent that they have some specific end, purpose, or result in mind, they have no real moral worth. Whatever value they have is extrinsic to the agent. For Kant, the only judgment that can have moral value, value that expresses intrinsic moral worth illustrative of a 'good will,' is an imperative, i.e., a moral command, that, since it is grounded in pure practical reason, has no exception and thus, may be said to be categorical. Thus, the *categorical imperative* expresses a moral command that any and all rational agents would choose insofar as their motives are grounded in duty toward and respect for the moral law.

To determine whether an action has moral worth we must, according to Kant, consider three things: first, there is *the act* itself. Second, there is the subjective principle which determines the action and which the action exemplifies, or what Kant calls *the maxim.* Consider, for example, the action of rescuing a person from a burning building. Here the maxim might be something like, "one should preserve human life whenever possible." This maxim is said to be a subjective principle inasmuch as it is freely chosen by the subject; it can be adopted, modified, and disposed of at the discretion of the individual. The third element involved in determining moral worth is what Kant calls *the moral law.* The moral law is said to be an objective principle of action insofar as it is necessarily and universally applicable to any and all moral agents regardless of their circumstances. In other words, what the moral law prescribes is what any rational moral agent would be compelled to do, *qua* rational moral agent. Since we are humans and are therefore subject to various less than rational desires and motives, our rational moral duty comes to us in terms of what we *ought* to do.

Like the first Critique, Kant's *Critique of Practical Reason* begins with our ordinary, common experience; in this case, our ordinary experience of making moral judgments. He now proceeds to ask the 'transcendental question': what are the necessary conditions for our having such experiences? The most fundamental condition for any and all morality is, of course, the assumption of freedom. Unless humans have free will, it makes no sense to ascribe moral blame or praise to an action. In earlier discussions (cf. the section of the first Critique entitled the Third Antinomy and in Section III of the *Foundations*), Kant illustrates what appears to be an irreparable contradiction regarding our conception of freedom. On the one hand, we see the world as a closed, deterministic system, and inasmuch as we are members of this system, human freedom seems to be impossible. On the other hand, insofar as we regard our own actions as originating from free choice, or spontaneity, and we ascribe moral blame or praise to such actions, then human freedom is a viable hypothesis. His solution to this antinomy is to assert that both claims are true; that we must see ourselves as members of *both* the mechanistic, phenomenal realm, *and* as members of a supersensible, noumenal realm of moral agency. Thus, human freedom becomes an idea of pure practical reason. As an idea, it cannot and need not be demonstrated in the realm of theoretical knowledge, in the domain of empirical experience. It is something that can be thought; it is something that can serve and must serve to organize our moral experience. It is a transcendental principle, or a necessary condition for the possibility of our having any moral experience whatsoever.

While the influences of Kant's rationalistic education have been evident throughout his writings, it is here, in the *Critique of Practical Reason* that we see evidence of the influence of his pietist side, or his desire "to deny knowledge, in order to make room for faith." In addition to freedom, Kant here contends that the ideas of God and the immortal soul should also be regarded as ideas of pure practical reason. Like freedom, such ideas are not susceptible to the rules of theoretical reason. Any attempts to demonstrate the existence of such things on the basis of empirical evidence or the traditional deductive models of proof are doomed to failure. Yet, such ideas can indeed be thought without contradiction. And furthermore, they can be usefully employed in our moral activity. In fact, Kant insists that they must so be employed.

The idea of moral goodness means, for Kant, actions done purely from duty. Such actions express a maxim, or subjective principle of action, that is consistent with the universal principle, or the moral law; the law that 'compels' all rational agents to do the morally good thing by informing us what we ought to do. By freely choosing to follow the recommendations of the moral law, the moral agent expresses, by his or her action, a 'good will' (i.e., an action grounded in the categorical imperative); a will that is not determined by desire, appetites, or results (i.e., an action grounded in a hypothetical imperative). Yet the notion of a mere transient moral goodness, one restricted to the confines of a mortal lifetime, is inconsistent with Kant's conception of a good will as an absolute, unqualified good. Thus, in Book II of the *Critique of Practical Reason*, he introduces the immortal human soul as a postulate of pure practical reason. The moral law is absolute and unchanging. And it is only by conceiving the moral agent as an infinitely enduring existence capable of making infinite moral progress that the notion of moral goodness becomes possible. Thus, the immortal soul is shown to be a transcendental, or necessary, condition for possibility of moral behavior.

Kant next turns to the more problematical notion of God. He had already shown that all of the traditional metaphysical proofs for the existence of God were, without exception, worthless and misleading. They were worthless to the extent that they misapplied the principles of theoretical reason beyond their proper sphere; and they were misleading insofar as they gave people the false impression that theology was a kind of 'science of God'; that elements of faith could be affirmed on the basis of experience or reason. Now, in Book II of the second *Critique*, Kant argues that, like the immortal soul, the idea of God should be acknowledged as a postulate of pure practical reason. He notes that our moral activity occurs in the phenomenal realm, the world of nature that is determined by causal necessity. And our morally good actions, i.e., those actions done from respect for the moral law, express moral goodness in the natural world. Therefore, the possibility of goodness is contained both in the moral law itself, insofar as it can determine my will, *qua* a 'good will,' and in the natural, phenomenal world itself, insofar as such a world contains the possibility of expressing good moral actions. Now for the transcendental question: what is the necessary condition for the possibility of such a situation? What could serve as the cause or explanation for both of these facts? Kant's answer is God. God can be understood as the author of the phenomenal world, as the Highest Good who instilled in the world the conditions of moral possibility; and as the source of the human will and the object of the will, the moral law – the rational object of all moral value. The idea of God then is no longer left in abeyance from the human condition. For Kant, God is now an object of what he calls 'rational faith.' Thus, Kant has fulfilled the promise he made in the first *Critique*'s introduction: "to deny knowledge, in order to make room for faith."

Dennis Sweet holds a Ph.D. in philosophy from the University of Iowa. He writes frequently on Kant, Heraclitus, and Nietzsche, and teaches philosophy and history at several colleges in Pittsburgh.

PREFACE TO THE FOURTH EDITION

In this edition some corrections have been made.

The Portrait prefixed is from a photograph of an oil-painting in the possession of Gräfe and Unzer, booksellers, of Königsberg. It is inferior, as a work of art, to the portrait engraved in the former edition; but as it represents Kant in the vigour of his age, and, unlike the former, has never appeared in any book, readers will probably be pleased with the substitution. I possess also a copy of a rare full-length silhouette, photographic copies of which can be supplied.

BOOK I

THE ANALYTIC OF PURE
PRACTICAL REASON

CHAPTER I

OF THE PRINCIPLES OF PURE
PRACTICAL REASON

§ 1.—DEFINITION

PRACTICAL *principles* are propositions which contain a general determination of the will, having under it several practical rules. They are subjective, or *Maxims*, when the condition is regarded by the subject as valid only for his own will, but are objective, or practical *laws*, when the condition is recognized as objective, that is, valid for the will of every rational being.

REMARK

Supposing that *pure* reason contains in itself a practical motive, that is, one adequate to determine the will, then there are practical laws; otherwise all practical principles will be mere maxims. In case the will of a rational being is pathologically affected, there may occur a conflict of the maxims with the practical laws recognized by itself. For example, one may make it his maxim to let no injury pass unrevenged, and yet he may see that this is not a practical law, but only his own maxim; that, on the contrary, regarded as being in one and the same maxim a rule for the will of every rational being, it must contradict itself. In natural philosophy the principles of what happens (*e.g.* the principle of equality of action

3

and reaction in the communication of motion) are at the same time laws of nature; for the use of reason there is theoretical, and determined by the nature of the object. In practical philosophy, *i.e.* that which has to do only with the grounds of determination of the will, the principles which a man makes for himself are not laws by which one is inevitably bound; because reason in practical matters has to do with the subject, namely, with the faculty of desire, the special character of which may occasion variety in the rule. The practical rule is always a product of reason, because it prescribes action as a means to the effect. But in the case of a being with whom reason does not of itself determine the will, this rule is an *imperative*, i.e. a rule characterized by "shall," which expresses the objective necessitation of the action, and signifies that if reason completely determined the will, the action would inevitably take place according to this rule. Imperatives, therefore, are objectively valid, and are quite distinct from maxims, which are subjective principles. The former either determine the conditions of the causality of the rational being as an efficient cause, *i.e.* merely in reference to the effect and the means of attaining it; or they determine the will only, whether it is adequate to the effect or not . The former would be hypothetical imperatives, and contain mere precepts of skill; the latter, on the contrary, would be categorical, and would alone be practical laws. Thus maxims are *principles*, but not *imperatives*. Imperatives themselves, however, when they are conditional (*i.e.* do not determine the will simply as will, but only in respect to a desired effect, that is, when they are hypothetical imperatives), are practical *precepts*, but not *laws*. Laws must be sufficient to determine the will as will, even before I ask whether I have power sufficient for a desired effect, or the means necessary to produce it; hence they are categorical: otherwise they are not laws at all, because the necessity is wanting, which, if it is to be practical, must be independent on conditions which are pathological, and are therefore only contingently connected with the will. Tell a man, for example, that he must be industrious and thrifty in youth, in order that he may not want in old age; this is a correct and important practical precept of the will. But it is easy to see that in this case the will is directed to something *else* which it is presupposed that it desires, and as to this desire, we must leave it to the actor himself whether he looks forward to other resources than those of his own acquisition, or does not expect to be old, or thinks that in case of future necessity he will be able to make shift with little. Reason, from which alone can spring a rule involving necessity, does, indeed, give necessity to this precept (else it would not be an imperative), but this is a necessity dependent on subjective conditions, and cannot be supposed in the same degree in all subjects. But that reason may give laws it is necessary that it should only need to presuppose *itself,* because rules are objectively and universally valid only when they hold without any contingent subjective conditions, which distinguish one rational being from another. Now tell a man that he should never make a deceitful promise, this is a rule which only concerns his will, whether the purposes he may have can be attained thereby or not; it is the volition only which is to be determined *à priori* by that rule. If now it is found that this rule is practically right, then it is a law, because it is a categorical imperative. Thus, practical laws refer to the will only, without considering what is attained by its causality, and we may disregard this latter (as belonging to the world of sense) in order to have them quite pure.

§ II.—THEOREM I

All practical principles which presuppose an object (matter) of the faculty of desire as the ground of determination of the will are empirical, and can furnish no practical laws.

By the matter of the faculty of desire I mean an object the realization of which is desired. Now, if the desire for this object *precedes* the practical rule, and is the condition of our making it a principle, then I say (*in the first place*) this principle is in that case wholly empirical, for then what determines the choice is the idea of an object, and that relation of this idea to the subject by which its faculty of desire is determined to its realization. Such a relation to the subject is called the *pleasure* in the realization of an object. This, then, must be presupposed as a condition of the possibility of determination of the will. But it is impossible to know *à priori* of any idea of an object whether it will be connected with *pleasure* or *pain*, or be indifferent. In such cases, therefore, the determining principle of the choice must be empirical, and, therefore, also the practical material principle which presupposes it as a condition.

In the second place, since susceptibility to a pleasure or pain can be known only empirically, and cannot hold in the same degree for all rational beings, a principle which is based on this subjective condition may serve indeed as a *maxim* for the subject which possesses this susceptibility, but not as a *law* even to him (because it is wanting in objective necessity, which must be recognized *à priori*); it follows, therefore, that such a principle can never furnish a practical law.

§ III.—THEOREM II

All material practical principles as such are of one and the same kind, and come under the general principle of self-love or private happiness.

Pleasure arising from the idea of the existence of a thing, in so far as it is to determine the desire of this thing, is founded on the *susceptibility* of the subject, since it *depends* on the presence of an object; hence it belongs to sense (feeling), and not to understanding, which expresses a relation of the idea *to an object* according to concepts, not to the subject according to feelings. It is, then, practical only in so far as the faculty of desire is determined by the sensation of agreeableness which the subject expects from the actual existence of the object. Now, a rational being's consciousness of the pleasantness of life uninterruptedly accompanying his whole existence is happiness; and the principle which makes this the supreme ground of determination of the will is the principle of self-love. All material principles, then, which place the determining ground of the will in the pleasure or pain to be received from the existence of any object are all of the same kind, inasmuch as they all belong to the principle of self-love or private happiness.

COROLLARY

All *material* practical rules place the determining principle of the will in the *lower desires,* and if there were no *purely formal* laws of the will adequate to determine it, then we could not admit *any higher desire* at all.

REMARK I

It is surprising that men, otherwise acute, can think it possible to distinguish between *higher* and *lower desires,* according as the ideas which are connected with the feeling of pleasure have their origin in the *senses* or in the *understanding*; for when we inquire what are the determining grounds of desire, and place them in some expected pleasantness, it is of no consequence whence the *idea* of this pleasing object is derived, but only how much it *pleases.* Whether an idea has its seat and source in the understanding or not, if it can only determine the choice by presupposing a feeling of pleasure in the subject, it follows that its capability of determining the choice depends altogether on the nature of the inner sense, namely, that this can be agreeably affected by it. However dissimilar ideas of objects may be, though they be ideas of the understanding, or even of the reason in contrast to ideas of sense, yet the feeling of pleasure, by means of which they constitute the determining principle of the will (the expected satisfaction which impels the activity to the production of the object), is of one and the same kind, not only inasmuch as it can only be known empirically, but also inasmuch as it affects one and the same vital force which manifests itself in the faculty of desire, and in this respect can only differ in degree from every other ground of determination. Otherwise, how could we compare in respect of *magnitude* two principles of determination, the ideas of which depend upon different faculties, so as to prefer that which affects the faculty of desire in the highest degree. The same man may return unread an instructive book which he cannot again obtain, in order not to miss a hunt; he may depart in the midst of a fine speech, in order not to be late for dinner; he may leave a rational conversation, such as he otherwise values highly, to take his place at the gaming-table; he may even repulse a poor man whom he at other times takes pleasure in benefiting, because he has only just enough money in his pocket to pay for his admission to the theatre. If the determination of his will rests on the feeling of the agreeableness or disagreeableness that he expects from any cause, it is all the same to him by what sort of ideas he will be affected. The only thing that concerns him, in order to decide his choice, is, how great, how long continued, how easily obtained, and how often repeated, this agreeableness is. Just as to the man who wants money to spend, it is all the same whether the gold was dug out of the mountain or washed out of the sand, provided it is everywhere accepted at the same value; so the man who cares only for the enjoyment of life does not ask whether the ideas are of the understanding or the senses, but only *how much* and *how great pleasure* they will give for the longest time. It is only those that would gladly deny to pure reason the power of determining the will, without the presupposition of any feeling, who could deviate so far from their own exposition as to describe as quite heterogeneous what they have themselves previously brought under one and the same principle . Thus, for example, it is observed that we can find pleasure in the mere *exercise of power,* in the consciousness of our strength of mind in overcoming obstacles which are opposed to our designs, in the culture of our mental talents, etc.; and we justly call these more refined pleasures and enjoyments, because they are more in our power than others; they do not wear out, but rather increase the capacity for further enjoyment of them, and while they delight they at the same time cultivate. But to say on this account that they determine the will in a different way, and not through sense, whereas the possibility of the pleasure presupposes a feeling for it implanted in us, which is the first condition of this satisfaction; this is just as when ignorant persons that like to dabble in metaphysics imagine matter so subtle, so super-subtle, that they almost make themselves giddy with it, and then think that in this way they have conceived it as a *spiritual* and yet extended being. If with *Epicurus* we make virtue determine the will only by means of the pleasure it promises, we cannot afterwards blame him for holding that this pleasure is of the same kind as those of the coarsest senses. For we have no reason whatever to charge him with holding that the ideas by which this feeling is excited in us belong merely to the bodily senses. As far as can be conjectured, he sought the source of many of them in the use of the higher cognitive faculty; but this did not prevent him, and could not prevent him, from holding on the principle above stated, that the pleasure itself which those intellectual ideas give us, and by which alone they can determine the will, is just of the same kind. *Consistency* is the highest obligation of a philosopher, and yet the most rarely found. The ancient Greek schools give us more examples of it than we find in our *syncretistic* age, in which a certain shallow and dishonest *system of compromise* of contradictory principles is devised, because it commends itself better to a public which is content to know something of everything and nothing thoroughly, so as to please every party.[1]

The principle of private happiness, however much understanding and reason may be used in it, cannot contain any other determining principles for the will than those which belong to the *lower* desires; and either there are no [higher][2] desires at all, or *pure* reason must of itself alone be practical: that is, it must be able to determine the will by the mere form of the practical rule without supposing any feeling, and consequently without any idea of the pleasant or unpleasant, which is the matter of the desire, and which is always an empirical condition of the principles. Then only, when reason of itself determines the will (not as the servant of the inclination), it is really a *higher* desire to which that which is pathologically determined is subordinate, and is really, and even specifically, distinct from the latter, so that even the slightest admixture of the motives of the latter impairs its strength and superiority; just as in a mathematical demonstration the least empirical condition would degrade and destroy its force and value. Reason, with its practical law, determines the will immediately, not by means of an intervening feeling of pleasure or pain, not even of pleasure in the law itself, and it is only because it can, as pure reason, be practical, that it is possible for it to be *legislative*.

REMARK II

To be happy is necessarily the wish of every finite rational being, and this, therefore, is inevitably a determining principle of its faculty of desire. For we are not in possession originally of satisfaction with our whole existence—a bliss which would imply a consciousness of our own independent self-sufficiency—this is a problem imposed upon us by our own finite nature, because we have wants, and these wants regard the matter of our desires, that is, something that is relative to a subjective feeling of pleasure or pain, which determines what we need in order to be satisfied with our condition. But just because this material principle of determination can only be empirically known by the subject, it is impossible to regard this problem as a law; for a law being objective must contain the *very same principle of determination* of the will in all cases and for all rational beings. For, although the notion of happiness is *in every case* the foundation of the practical relation of the *objects* to the desires, yet it is only a general name for the subjective determining principles, and determines nothing specifically; whereas this is what alone we are concerned with in this practical problem, which cannot be solved at all without such specific determination. For it is every man's own special feeling of pleasure and pain that decides in what he is to place his happi-

ness, and even in the same subject this will vary with the difference of his wants according as this feeling changes, and thus a law
which is *subjectively necessary* (as a law of nature) is *objectively* a very
contingent practical principle, which can and must be very different in different subjects, and therefore can never furnish a law;
since, in the desire for happiness it is not the form (of conformity
to law) that is decisive, but simply the matter, namely, whether I
am to expect pleasure in following the law, and how much.
Principles of self-love may, indeed, contain universal precepts of
skill (how to find means to accomplish one's purposes), but in
that case they are merely theoretical principles;[3] as, for example,
how he who would like to eat bread should contrive a mill; but
practical precepts founded on them can never be universal, for
the determining principle of the desire is based on the feeling of
pleasure and pain, which can never be supposed to be universally
directed to the same objects.

Even supposing, however, that all finite rational beings were
thoroughly agreed as to what were the objects of their feelings of
pleasure and pain, and also as to the means which they must
employ to attain the one and avoid the other; still, they could *by no
means* set up the *principle of self-love* as a *practical law*, for this unanimity itself would be only contingent. The principle of determination would still be only subjectively valid and merely empirical,
and would not possess the necessity which is conceived in every
law, namely, an objective necessity arising from *à priori* grounds;
unless, indeed, we hold this necessity to be not at all practical, but
merely physical, viz. that our action is as inevitably determined by
our inclination, as yawning when we see others yawn. It would be
better to maintain that there are no practical laws at all, but only
counsels for the service of our desires, than to raise merely subjective principles to the rank of practical laws, which have objective
necessity, and not merely subjective, and which must be known by
reason *à priori*, not by experience (however empirically universal
this may be). Even the rules of corresponding phenomena are
only called laws of nature (*e.g.* the mechanical laws), when we

either know them really *à priori,* or (as in the case of chemical laws) suppose that they would be known *à priori* from objective grounds if our insight reached further. But in the case of merely subjective practical principles, it is expressly made a condition that they rest not on objective but on subjective conditions of choice, and hence that they must always be represented as mere maxims; never as practical laws. This second remark seems at first sight to be mere verbal refinement, but it defines[4] the terms of the most important distinction which can come into consideration in practical investigations.

§ IV.—Theorem III

A rational being cannot regard his maxims as practical universal laws, unless he conceives them as principles which determine the will, not by their matter, but by their form only.

By the matter of a practical principle I mean the object of the will. This object is either the determining ground of the will or it is not. In the former case the rule of the will is subjected to an empirical condition (viz. the relation of the determining idea to the feeling of pleasure and pain); consequently it cannot be a practical law. Now, when we abstract from a law all matter, *i.e.* every object of the will (as a determining principle), nothing is left but the mere *form* of a universal legislation. Therefore, either a rational being cannot conceive his subjective practical principles, that is, his maxims, as being at the same time universal laws, or he must suppose that their mere form, by which they are fitted for universal legislation, is alone what makes them practical laws.

REMARK

The commonest understanding can distinguish without instruction what form of maxim is adapted for universal legislation, and what is not. Suppose, for example, that I have made it my maxim to increase my fortune by every safe means. Now, I have a deposit in my hands, the owner of which is dead and has left no writing about it. This is just the case for my maxim. I desire, then, to know whether that maxim can also hold good as a universal practical law. I apply it, therefore, to the present case, and ask whether it could take the form of a law, and consequently whether I can by my maxim at the same time give such a law as this, that everyone may deny a deposit of which no one can produce a proof. I at once become aware that such a principle, viewed as a law, would annihilate itself, because the result would be that there would be no deposits. A practical law which I recognize as such must be qualified for universal legislation; this is an identical proposition, and therefore self-evident. Now, if I say that my will is subject to a practical law, I cannot adduce my inclination (*e.g.* in the present case my avarice) as a principle of determination fitted to be a universal practical law; for this is so far from being fitted for a universal legislation that, if put in the form of a universal law, it would destroy itself.

It is, therefore, surprising that intelligent men could have thought of calling the desire of happiness a universal *practical law* on the ground that the desire is universal, and, therefore, also the *maxim* by which everyone makes this desire determine his will. For whereas in other cases a universal law of nature makes everything harmonious; here, on the contrary, if we attribute to the maxim the universality of a law, the extreme opposite of harmony will follow, the greatest opposition, and the complete destruction of the maxim itself, and its purpose. For, in that case, the will of all has not one and the same object, but everyone has his own (his private welfare), which may accidentally accord with the purposes of others which are equally selfish, but it is far from sufficing for a law; because the occasional exceptions which one is permitted to make are endless, and cannot be definitely embraced in one universal rule. In this manner, then, results a harmony like that which a certain satirical poem depicts as existing between a married couple bent on going to ruin, "O, marvellous harmony, what he wishes, she wishes also"; or like what is said of the pledge of Francis I to the Emperor

Charles V, "What my brother Charles wishes that I wish also" (viz. Milan). Empirical principles of determination are not fit for any universal external legislation, but just as little for internal; for each man makes his own subject the foundation of his inclination, and in the same subject sometimes one inclination, sometimes another, has the preponderance. To discover a law which would govern them all under this condition, namely, bringing them all into harmony, is quite impossible.

§ V.—PROBLEM I

Supposing that the mere legislative form of maxims is alone the sufficient determining principle of a will, to find the nature of the will which can be determined by it alone.

Since the bare form of the law can only be conceived by reason, and is, therefore, not an object of the senses, and consequently does not belong to the class of phenomena, it follows that the idea of it, which determines the will, is distinct from all the principles that determine events in nature according to the law of causality, because in their case the determining principles must themselves be phenomena. Now, if no other determining principle can serve as a law for the will except that universal legislative form, such a will must be conceived as quite independent on the natural law of phenomena in their mutual relation, namely, the law of causality; such independence is called *freedom* in the strictest, that is in the transcendental sense; consequently, a will which can have its law in nothing but the mere legislative form of the maxim is a free will.

§ VI.—PROBLEM II

Supposing that a will is free, to find the law which alone is competent to determine it necessarily.

Since the matter of the practical law, *i.e.* an object of the maxim, can never be given otherwise than empirically, and the free will is independent on empirical conditions (that is, conditions belonging to the world of sense), and yet is determinable, consequently a free will must find its principle of determination in the law, and yet independently of the matter of the law. But, beside the matter of the law, nothing is contained in it except the legislative form. It is the legislative form, then, contained in the maxim, which can alone constitute a principle of determination of the [free] will.

REMARKS

Thus freedom and an unconditional practical law reciprocally imply each other. Now I do not ask here whether they are in fact distinct, or whether an unconditional law is not rather merely the consciousness of a pure practical reason, and the latter identical with the positive concept of freedom; I only ask, whence *begins* our *knowledge* of the unconditionally practical, whether it is from freedom or from the practical law? Now it cannot begin from freedom, for of this we cannot be immediately conscious, since the first concept of it is negative; nor can we infer it from experience, for experience gives us the knowledge only of the law of phenomena, and hence of the mechanism of nature, the direct opposite of freedom. It is therefore the moral law, of which we become directly conscious (as soon as we trace for ourselves maxims of the will), that *first* presents itself to us, and leads directly to the concept of freedom, inasmuch as reason presents it as a principle of determination not to be outweighed by any sensible conditions, nay, wholly independent of them. But how is the consciousness of that moral law possible? We can become conscious of pure practical laws just as we are conscious of pure theoretical principles, by attending to the necessity with which reason prescribes them, and to the elimination of all empirical conditions, which it directs. The concept of a pure will arises out of the former, as that of a pure understanding arises out of the latter. That this is the true subordination of our concepts, and that it is morality that first discovers to us the notion of freedom, hence that it is *practical reason* which, with this concept, first proposes to speculative reason the most insoluble problem, thereby placing it in the greatest perplexity, is evident from the following consideration:—Since nothing in phenomena can be explained by the concept of freedom, but the mechanism of nature must constitute the only clue; moreover, when pure reason tries to ascend in the series of causes to the unconditioned, it falls into an antinomy which is entangled in incomprehensibilities on the one side as much as the other; whilst the latter (namely, mechanism) is at least useful in the explanation of phenomena, therefore no one would ever have been so rash as to introduce freedom into science, had not the moral law, and with it practical reason, come in and forced this notion upon us. Experience, however, confirms this order of notions. Suppose some one asserts of his lustful appetite that, when the desired object and the opportunity are present, it is quite irresistible. [Ask him]—if a gallows were erected before the house where he finds this opportunity, in order that he should be hanged thereon immediately after the gratification of his lust, whether he could not then control his passion; we need not be long in doubt what he would reply. Ask him, however—if his sovereign ordered him, on pain of the same immediate execution, to bear false witness against an honourable man, whom the prince might wish to destroy under a plausible pretext, would he consider it possible in that case to overcome his love of life, however great it may be. He would perhaps not venture to affirm whether he would do so or not, but he must unhesitatingly admit that it is possible to do so. He judges, therefore, that he can do a certain thing because he is conscious that he ought, and he recognizes that he is free—a fact which but for the moral law he would never have known.

§ VII.—FUNDAMENTAL LAW OF THE PURE PRACTICAL REASON

Act so that the maxim of thy will can always at the same time hold good as a principle of universal legislation.

REMARK

Pure geometry has postulates which are practical propositions, but contain nothing further than the assumption that we *can* do something if it is required that we *should* do it, and these are the only geometrical propositions that concern actual existence. They are, then, practical rules under a problematical condition of the will; but here the rule says:—We absolutely must proceed in a certain manner. The practical rule is, therefore, unconditional, and hence it is conceived *à priori* as a categorically practical proposition by which the will is objectively determined absolutely and immediately (by the practical rule itself, which thus is in this case a law); for *pure reason practical of itself* is here directly legislative. The will is thought as independent on empirical conditions, and, therefore, as pure will determined by *the mere form of the law,* and this principle of determination is regarded as the supreme condition of all maxims. The thing is strange enough, and has no parallel in all the rest of our practical knowledge. For the *à priori* thought of a possible universal legislation which is therefore merely problematical, is unconditionally commanded as a law without borrowing anything from experience or from any external will. This, however, is not a precept to do something by which some desired effect can be attained (for then the will would depend on physical conditions), but a rule that determines the will *à priori* only so far as regards the forms of its maxims; and thus it is at least not impossible to conceive that a law, which only applies to the *subjective* form of principles, yet serves as a principle of determination by means of the *objective* form of law in general. We may call the consciousness of this fundamental law a fact of reason, because we cannot reason it out from antecedent data of reason, *e.g.* the consciousness of freedom (for this is not antecedently given), but it forces itself on us as a synthetic *à priori* proposition, which is not based on any intuition, either pure or empirical. It would, indeed, be analytical if the freedom of the will were presupposed, but to presuppose freedom as a positive *concept* would require an intellectual intuition, which cannot here be assumed; however, when we regard this law as *given*, it must be observed, in order not to fall into any misconception, that it is not an empirical fact, but the sole fact of the pure reason, which thereby announces itself as originally legislative (*sic volo sic jubeo*).

COROLLARY

Pure reason is practical of itself alone, and gives (to man) a universal law which we call the *Moral Law.*

REMARK

The fact just mentioned is undeniable. It is only necessary to analyse the judgment that men pass on the lawfulness of their actions, in order to find that, whatever inclination may say to the contrary, reason, incorruptible and self-constrained, always confronts the maxim of the will in any action with the pure will, that is, with itself, considering itself as *à priori* practical. Now this principle of morality, just on account of the universality of the legislation which makes it the formal supreme determining principle of the will, without regard to any subjective differences, is declared by the reason to be a law for all rational beings, in so far as they have a will, that is, a power to determine their causality by the conception of rules; and, therefore, so far as they are capable of acting according to principles, and consequently also according to practical *à priori* principles (for these alone have the necessity that reason requires in a principle). It is, therefore, not limited to men only, but applies to all finite beings that possess reason and will; nay, it even includes the Infinite Being as the supreme intelligence. In the former case, however, the law has the form of an imperative, because in them, as rational beings, we can suppose a *pure* will, but being creatures affected with wants and physical motives, not a *holy* will, that is, one which would be incapable of any maxim conflicting with the moral law. In their case, therefore, the moral law is an *imperative*, which commands categorically, because the law is unconditioned; the relation of such a will to this law is *dependence* under the name of *obligation*, which implies a *constraint* to an action, though only by reason and its objective law; and this action is called *duty*, because an elective will, subject to pathological affections (though not determined by them, and therefore still free), implies a wish that arises from *subjective* causes, and therefore may often be opposed to the pure objective determining principle; whence it requires the moral constraint of a resistance of the practical reason, which may be called an internal, but intellectual, compulsion. In the supreme intelligence the elective will is rightly conceived as incapable of any maxim which could not at the same time be objectively a law; and the notion of *holiness*, which on that account belongs to it, places it, not indeed above all practical laws, but above all practically restrictive laws, and consequently above obligation and duty. This holiness of will is, however, a practical idea, which must necessarily serve as a type to which finite rational beings can only approximate indefinitely, and which the pure moral law, which is itself on this account called holy, constantly and rightly holds before their eyes. The utmost that finite practical reason can effect is to be certain of this indefinite progress of one's maxims, and of their steady disposition to advance. This is virtue, and virtue, at least as a naturally acquired faculty, can never be perfect, because assurance in such a case never becomes apodictic certainty, and when it only amounts to persuasion is very dangerous.

§ VIII.—THEOREM IV

The *autonomy* of the will is the sole principle of all moral laws, and of all duties which conform to them; on the other hand, *heteronomy* of the elective will not only cannot be the basis of any obligation, but is, on the contrary, opposed to the principle thereof, and to the morality of the will.

In fact the sole principle of morality consists in the independence on all matter of the law (namely, a desired object), and in the determination of the elective will by the mere universal legislative form of which its maxim must be capable. Now this *independence* is *freedom* in the *negative* sense, and this *self-legislation* of the pure, and therefore practical, reason is freedom in the *positive* sense. Thus the moral law expresses nothing else than the *autonomy* of the pure practical reason; that is, freedom; and this is itself the formal condition of all maxims, and on this condition only can they agree with the supreme practical law. If therefore the matter of the volition, which can be nothing else than the object of a desire that is connected with the law, enters into the practical law, *as the condition of its possibility*, there results heteronomy of the elective will, namely, dependence on the physical law that we should follow some impulse or inclination. In that case the will does not give itself the law, but only the precept how rationally to follow pathological law; and the maxim which, in such a case, never contains the universally legislative form, not only produces no obligation, but is itself opposed to the principle of a pure practical reason, and, therefore, also to the moral disposition, even though the resulting action may be conformable to the law.

REMARK I

Hence a practical precept, which contains a material (and therefore empirical) condition, must never be reckoned a practical law. For the law of the pure will, which is free, brings the will into a sphere quite different from the empirical; and as the necessity involved in the law is not a physical necessity, it can only consist in the formal conditions of the possibility of a law in general. All the matter of practical rules rests on subjective conditions, which give them only a conditional universality (in case I *desire* this or that, what I must do in order to obtain it), and they all turn on the principle of *private happiness*. Now, it is indeed undeniable that every volition must have an object, and therefore a matter; but it does not follow that this is the determining principle, and the condition of the maxim; for, if it is so, then this cannot be exhibited in a universally legislative form, since in that case the expectation of the existence of the object would be the determining cause of the choice, and the volition must presuppose the dependence of the faculty of desire on the existence of something; but this dependence can only be sought in empirical conditions, and therefore can never furnish a foundation for a necessary and universal rule. Thus, the happiness of others may be the object of the will of a rational being. But if it were the determining principle of the maxim, we must assume that we find not only a rational satisfaction in the welfare of others, but also a want such as the sympathetic disposition in some men occasions. But I cannot assume the existence of this want in every rational being (not at all in God). The matter, then, of the maxim may remain, but it must not be the condition of it, else the maxim could not be fit for a law. Hence, the mere form of law, which limits the matter, must also be a reason for adding this matter to the will, not for presupposing it. For example, let the matter be my own happiness. This (rule), if I attribute it to everyone (as, in fact, I may, in the case of every finite being), can become an *objective* practical law only if I include the happiness of others. Therefore, the law that we should promote the happiness of others does not arise from the assumption that this is an object of everyone's choice, but merely from this, that the form of universality which reason requires as the condition of giving to a maxim of self-love the objective validity of a law, is the principle that determines the will. Therefore it was not the object (the happiness of others) that determined the pure will, but it was the form of law only, by which I restricted my maxim, founded on inclination, so as to give it the universality of a law, and thus to adapt it to the practical reason; and it is this restriction alone, and not the addition of an external spring, that can give rise to the notion of the *obligation* to extend the maxim of my self-love to the happiness of others.

REMARK II

The direct opposite of the principle of morality is, when the principle of *private* happiness is made the determining principle of the will, and with this is to be reckoned, as I have shown above, everything that places the determining principle which is to serve as a law anywhere but in the legislative form of the maxim. This contradiction, however, is not merely logical, like that which would arise between rules empirically conditioned, if they were raised to the rank of necessary principles of cognition, but is practical, and would ruin morality altogether were not the voice of reason in reference to the will so clear, so irrepressible, so distinctly audible even to the commonest men. It can only, indeed, be maintained in the perplexing speculations of the schools, which are bold enough to shut their ears against that heavenly voice, in order to support a theory that costs no trouble.

Suppose that an acquaintance whom you otherwise liked were to attempt to justify himself to you for having borne false witness, first by alleging the, in his view, sacred duty of consulting his own happiness; then by enumerating the advantages which he had gained thereby, pointing out the prudence he had shown in securing himself against detection, even by yourself, to whom he now reveals the secret only in order that he may be able to deny it at any time; and suppose he were then to affirm, in all seriousness, that he has fulfilled a true human duty; you would either laugh in his face, or shrink back from him with disgust; and yet, if a man has regulated his principles of action solely with a view to his own advantage, you would have nothing whatever to object against this mode of proceeding. Or suppose some one recommends you a man as steward, as a man to whom you can blindly trust all your affairs; and, in order to inspire you with confidence, extols him as a prudent man who thoroughly understands his own interest, and is so indefatigably active that he lets slip no opportunity of advancing it; lastly, lest you should be afraid of finding a vulgar selfishness in him, praises the good taste with which he lives: not seeking his pleasure in money-making, or in coarse wantonness, but in the enlargement of his knowledge, in instructive intercourse with a select circle, and even in relieving the needy; while as to the means (which, of course, derive all their value from the end) he is not particular, and is ready to use other people's money for the purpose, as if it were his own, provided only he knows that he can do so safely and without discovery; you would either believe that the recommender was mocking you, or that he had lost his senses. So sharply and clearly marked are the boundaries of morality and self-love that even the commonest eye cannot fail to distinguish whether a thing belongs to the one or the other. The few remarks that follow may appear superfluous where the truth is so plain, but at least they may serve to give a little more distinctness to the judgment of common sense.

The principle of happiness may, indeed, furnish maxims, but never such as would be competent to be laws of the will, even if *universal* happiness were made the object. For since the knowledge of this rests on mere empirical data, since every man's judgment on it depends very much on his particular point of view, which is itself moreover very variable, it can supply only *general* rules, not *universal*; that is, it can give rules which on the average will most frequently fit, but not rules which must hold good always and necessarily; hence, no practical *laws* can be founded on it. Just because in this case an object of choice is the foundation of the rule, and must therefore precede it; the rule can refer to nothing but what is [felt]⁵, and therefore it refers to experience and is founded on it, and then the variety of judgment must be endless. This principle, therefore, does not prescribe the same practical rules to all rational beings, although the rules are all included under a common title, namely, that of happiness. The moral law, however, is conceived as objectively necessary, only because it holds for everyone that has reason and will.

The maxim of self-love (prudence) only *advises*; the law of morality *commands*. Now there is a great difference between that which we are *advised* to do and that to which we are *obliged*.

The commonest intelligence can easily and without hesitation see what, on the principle of autonomy of the will, requires to be done; but on supposition of heteronomy of the will, it is hard and requires knowledge of the world to see what is to be done. That is to say, what *duty* is, is plain of itself to everyone; but what is to bring true durable advantage, such as will extend to the whole of one's existence, is always veiled in impenetrable obscurity; and much prudence is required to adapt the practical rule founded on it to the ends of life, even tolerably, by making proper exceptions. But the moral law commands the most punctual obedience from everyone; it must, therefore, not be so difficult to judge what it requires to be done, that the commonest unpractised understanding, even without worldly prudence, should fail to apply it rightly.

It is always in everyone's power to satisfy the categorical command of morality; whereas it is but seldom possible, and by no means so to everyone, to satisfy the empirically conditioned precept of happiness, even with regard to a single purpose. The reason is, that in the former case there is question only of the maxim, which must be genuine and pure; but in the latter case there is question also of one's capacity and physical power to realize a desired object. A command that everyone should try to make himself happy would be foolish, for one never commands anyone to do what he of himself infallibly wishes to do. We must only command the means, or rather supply them, since he cannot do everything that he wishes. But to command morality under the name of duty is quite rational; for, in the first place, not everyone is willing to obey its precepts if they oppose his inclinations; and as to the means of obeying this law, these need not in this case be taught, for in this respect whatever he wishes to do he can do.

He who has *lost* at play may be *vexed* at himself and his folly; but if he is conscious of having *cheated* at play (although he has gained thereby), he must *despise* himself as soon as he compares himself with the moral law. This must, therefore, be something different from the principle of private happiness. For a man must have a different criterion when he is compelled to say to himself: I am a *worthless* fellow, though I have filled my purse; and when he approves himself, and says: I am a *prudent* man, for I have enriched my treasure.

Finally, there is something further in the idea of our practical reason, which accompanies the transgression of a moral law— namely, its *ill desert*. Now the notion of punishment, as such, cannot be united with that of becoming a partaker of happiness; for although he who inflicts the punishment may at the same time have the benevolent purpose of directing this punishment to this end, yet it must first be justified in itself as punishment, *i.e.* as mere harm, so that if it stopped there, and the person punished could get no glimpse of kindness hidden behind this harshness, he must yet admit that justice was done him, and that his reward was perfectly suitable to his conduct. In every punishment, as such, there must first be justice, and this constitutes the essence of the notion. Benevolence may, indeed, be united with it, but the man who has deserved punishment, has not the least reason to reckon upon this. Punishment, then, is a physical evil, which, though it be not connected with moral evil as a *natural* consequence, ought to be connected with it as a consequence by the principles of a moral legislation. Now, if every crime, even without regarding the physical consequence with respect to the actor, is in itself punishable, that is, forfeits happiness (at least partially), it is obviously absurd to say that the crime consisted just in this, that he has drawn punishment on himself, thereby injuring his private happiness (which, on the principle of self-love, must be the proper notion of all crime). According to this view the punishment would be the reason for calling anything a crime, and justice would, on the contrary, consist in omitting all punishment, and even preventing that which naturally follows; for, if this were done, there would no longer be any evil in the action, since the harm which otherwise followed it, and on account of which alone the action was called evil, would now be prevented. To look, however, on all rewards and punishments as merely the machinery in the hand of a higher power, which is to serve only to set rational creatures striving after their final end (happiness), this is to reduce the will to a mechanism destructive of freedom; this is so evident that it need not detain us.

More refined, though equally false, is the theory of those who suppose a certain special moral sense, which sense and not reason determines the moral law, and in consequence of which the consciousness of virtue is supposed to be directly connected with contentment and pleasure; that of vice, with mental dissatisfaction and pain; thus reducing the whole to the desire of private happiness. Without repeating what has been said above, I will here only remark the fallacy they fall into. In order to imagine the vicious man as tormented with mental dissatisfaction by the consciousness of his transgressions, they must first represent him as in the main basis of his character, at least in some degree, morally good; just as he who is pleased with the consciousness of right conduct must be conceived as already virtuous. The notion of morality and duty must, therefore, have preceded any regard to this satisfaction, and cannot be derived from it. A man must first appreciate the importance of what we call duty, the authority of the moral law, and the immediate dignity which the following of it gives to the person in his own eyes, in order to feel that satisfaction in the consciousness of his conformity to it, and the bitter remorse that accompanies the consciousness of its transgression. It is, therefore, impossible to feel this satisfaction or dissatisfaction prior to the knowledge of obligation, or to make it the basis of the latter. A man must be at least half honest in order even to be able to form a conception of these feelings. I do not deny that as the human will is, by virtue of liberty, capable of being immediately determined by the moral law, so frequent practice in accordance with this principle of determination can, at last, produce subjectively a feeling of satisfaction; on the contrary, it is a duty to establish and to cultivate this, which alone deserves to be called properly the moral feeling; but the notion of duty cannot be derived from it, else we should have to suppose a feeling for the law as such, and thus make that an object of sensation which can only be thought by the reason; and this, if it is not to be a flat contradiction, would destroy all notion of duty, and put in its place a mere mechanical play of refined inclinations sometimes contending with the coarser.

If now we compare our *formal* supreme principle of pure practical reason (that of autonomy of the will) with all previous *material* principles of morality, we can exhibit them all in a table in which all possible cases are exhausted, except the one formal principle; and thus we can show visibly that it is vain to look for any other principle than that now proposed. In fact all possible principles of determination of the will are either merely *subjective*, and therefore empirical, or are also *objective* and rational; and both are either *external* or *internal*.

Practical Material Principles of Determination taken as the Foundation of Morality, are:—

SUBJECTIVE.		OBJECTIVE.	
EXTERNAL.	INTERNAL.	EXTERNAL.	INTERNAL.
Education.	Physical feeling.	Perfection.	Will of God.
(*Montaigne.*)	(*Epicurus.*)	(*Wolf* and the	(*Crusius* and other
The civil	Moral feeling.	Stoics.)	theological
Constitution.	(*Hutcheson*)		Moralists.)
(*Mandeville.*)			

Those at the left hand are all empirical, and evidently incapable of furnishing the universal principle of morality; but those on the right hand are based on reason (for perfection as a quality of things, and the highest perfection conceived as *substance*, that is, God, can only be thought by means of rational concepts). But the former notion, namely, that of *perfection*, may either be taken in a *theoretic* signification, and then it means nothing but the completeness of each thing in its own kind (transcendental), or that of a thing, merely as a thing (metaphysical); and with that we are not concerned here. But the notion of perfection in a *practical* sense is the fitness or sufficiency of a thing for all sorts of purposes. This perfection, as a *quality* of man, and consequently internal, is nothing but *talent*, and, what strengthens or completes this, *skill*. Supreme perfection conceived as *substance*, that is, God, and consequently external (considered practically), is the sufficiency of this being for all ends. Ends then must first be given, relatively to which only can the notion of *perfection* (whether internal in ourselves or external in God) be the determining principle of the will. But an end—being an *object* which must precede the determination of the will by a practical rule, and contain the ground of the possibility of this determination, and therefore contain also the matter of the will, taken as its determining principle—such an end is always empirical, and, therefore, may serve for the *Epicurean* principle of the happiness theory, but not for the pure rational principle of morality and duty. Thus, talents and the improvement of them, because they contribute to the advantages of life; or the will of God, if agreement with it be taken as the object of the will, without any antecedent independent practical principle, can be motives only by reason of the *happiness* expected therefrom. Hence it follows, *first*, that all the principles here stated are *material*; *secondly*, that they include all possible material principles; and, finally, the conclusion, that since material principles are quite incapable of furnishing the supreme moral law (as has been shown), the *formal practical principle* of the pure reason (according to which the mere form of a universal legislation must constitute the supreme and immediate determining principle of the will) is the *only* one *possible* which is adequate to furnish categorical imperatives; that is, practical laws (which make actions a duty); and in general to serve as the principle of morality, both in criticizing conduct and also in its application to the human will to determine it.

I.—*Of the Deduction of the Fundamental Principles of the Pure Practical Reason*

This Analytic shows that pure reason can be practical, that is, can of itself determine the will independently of anything empirical; and this it proves by a fact in which pure reason in us proves itself actually practical, namely, the autonomy shown in the fundamental principle of morality, by which reason determines the will to action.

It shows at the same time that this fact is inseparably connected with the consciousness of freedom of the will; nay, is identical with it; and by this the will of a rational being, although as belonging to the world of sense it recognizes itself as necessarily subject to the laws of causality like other efficient causes; yet, at the same time, on another side, namely, as a being in itself, is conscious of existing in and being determined by an intelligible order of things; conscious not by virtue of a special intuition of itself, but by virtue of certain dynamical laws which determine its causality in the sensible world; for it has been elsewhere proved that if freedom is predicated of us, it transports us into an intelligible order of things.

Now, if we compare with this the analytical part of the critique of pure speculative reason, we shall see a remarkable contrast. There it was not fundamental principles, but pure, sensible *intuition* (space and time), that was the first *datum* that made *à priori* knowledge possible, though only of objects of the senses. Synthetical principles could not be derived from mere concepts without intuition; on the contrary, they could only exist with reference to this intuition, and therefore to objects of possible experience, since it is the concepts of the understanding, united with this intuition, which alone make that knowledge possible which we call experience. Beyond objects of experience, and therefore with regard to things as noumena, all positive knowledge was rightly disclaimed for speculative reason. This reason, however, went so far as to establish with certainty the concept of noumena; that is, the possibility, nay, the necessity, of thinking them; for example, it showed against all objections that the supposition of freedom, negatively considered, was quite consistent with those principles and limitations of pure theoretic reason. But it could not give us any definite enlargement of our knowledge with respect to such objects, but, on the contrary, cut off all view of them altogether.

On the other hand, the moral law, although it gives no *view*, yet gives us a fact absolutely inexplicable from any data of the sensible world, and the whole compass of our theoretical use of reason, a fact which points to a pure world of the understanding, nay, even defines it *positively*, and enables us to know something of it, namely, a law.

This law (as far as rational beings are concerned) gives to the world of sense, which is a sensible system of nature, the form of a world of the understanding, that is, of a *supersensible system of nature*, without interfering with its mechanism. Now, a system of nature, in the most general sense, is the existence of things under laws. The sensible nature of rational beings in general is their existence under laws empirically conditioned, which, from the point of view of reason, is *heteronomy*. The supersensible nature of the same beings, on the other hand, is their existence according to laws which are independent on every empirical condition, and therefore belong to the *autonomy* of pure reason. And, since the laws by which the existence of things depends on cognition are practical, supersensible nature, so far as we can form any notion of it, is nothing else than a *system of nature under the autonomy of pure practical reason*. Now, the law of this autonomy is the moral law, which, therefore, is the fundamental law of a supersensible nature, and of a pure world of understanding, whose counterpart must exist in the world of sense, but without interfering with its laws. We might call the former the *archetypal* world (*natura archetypa*), which we only know in the reason; and the latter the *ectypal* world (*natura ectypa*), because it contains the possible effect of the idea of the former which is the determining principle of the will. For the moral law, in fact, transfers us ideally into a system in which pure reason, if it were accompanied with adequate physical power, would produce the *summum bonum*, and it determines our will to give the sensible world the form of a system of rational beings.[6]

The least attention to oneself proves that this idea really serves as a model for the determinations of our will.

When the maxim which I am disposed to follow in giving testimony is tested by the practical reason, I always consider what it would be if it were to hold as a universal law of nature. It is manifest that in this view it would oblige everyone to speak the truth. For it cannot hold as a universal law of nature that statements should be allowed to have the force of proof, and yet to be purposely untrue. Similarly, the maxim which I adopt with respect to disposing freely of my life is at once determined, when I ask myself what it should be, in order that a system, of which it is the law, should maintain itself. It is obvious that in such a system no one could *arbitrarily* put an end to his own life, for such an arrangement would not be a permanent order of things. And so in all similar cases. Now, in nature, as it actually is an object of experience, the free will is not of itself determined to maxims which could of themselves be the foundation of a natural system of universal laws, or which could even be adapted to a system so constituted; on the contrary, its maxims are private inclinations which constitute, indeed, a natural whole in conformity with pathological (physical) laws, but could not form part of a system of nature, which would only be possible through our will acting in accordance with pure practical laws. Yet we are, through reason, conscious of a law to which all our maxims are subject, as though a natural order must be originated from our will. This law, therefore, must be the idea of a natural system not given in experience, and yet possible through freedom; a system, therefore, which is supersensible, and to which we give objective reality, at least in a practical point of view, since we look on it as an object of our will as pure rational beings.

Hence the distinction between the laws of a natural system to which the *will is subject,* and of a natural system which is *subject to a will* (as far as its relation to its free actions is concerned), rests on this, that in the former the objects must be causes of the ideas which determine the will; whereas in the latter the will is the cause of the objects; so that its causality has its determining principle solely in the pure faculty of reason, which may therefore be called a pure practical reason.

There are therefore two very distinct problems: how, on *the one side,* pure reason can *cognise* objects *à priori,* and how *on the other side* it can be an immediate determining principle of the will, that is, of the causality of the rational being with respect to the reality of objects (through the mere thought of the universal validity of its own maxims as laws).

The former, which belongs to the critique of the pure speculative reason, requires a previous explanation, how intuitions without which no object can be given, and, therefore, none known synthetically, are possible *à priori*; and its solution turns out to be that these are all only sensible, and therefore do not render possible any speculative knowledge which goes further than possible experience reaches; and that therefore all the principles of that pure speculative[7] reason avail only to make experience possible; either experience of given objects or of those that may be given *ad infinitum*, but never are completely given.

The latter, which belongs to the critique of practical reason, requires no explanation how the objects of the faculty of desire are possible, for that being a problem of the theoretical knowledge of nature is left to the critique of the speculative reason, but only how reason can determine the maxims of the will; whether this takes place only by means of empirical ideas as principles of determination, or whether pure reason can be practical and be the law of a possible order of nature, which is not empirically knowable. The possibility of such a supersensible system of nature, the conception of which can also be the ground of its reality through our own free will, does not require any *à priori* intuition (of an intelligible world) which, being in this case supersensible, would be impossible for us. For the question is only as to the determining principle of volition in its maxims, namely, whether it is empirical, or is a conception of the pure reason (having the legal character belonging to it in general), and how it can be the latter. It is left to the theoretic principles of reason to decide whether the causality of the will suffices for the realization of the objects or not, this being an inquiry into the possibility of the objects of the volition. Intuition of these objects is therefore of no importance to the practical problem. We are here concerned only with the determination of the will and the determining principles of its maxims as a free will, not at all with the result. For, provided only that the *will* conforms to the law of pure reason, then let its *power* in execution be what it may, whether according to these maxims of legislation of a possible system of nature any such system really results or not, this is no concern of the critique, which only inquires whether, and in what way, pure reason can be practical, that is directly determine the will.

In this inquiry criticism may and must begin with pure practical laws and their reality. But instead of intuition it takes as their foundation the conception of their existence in the intelligible world, namely, the concept of freedom. For this concept has no other meaning, and these laws are only possible in relation to freedom of the will; but freedom being supposed, they are necessary; or conversely freedom is necessary because those laws are necessary, being practical postulates. It cannot be further explained how this consciousness of the moral law, or, what is the same thing, of freedom, is possible; but that it is admissible is well established in the theoretical critique.

The *Exposition* of the supreme principle of practical reason is now finished; that is to say, it has been shown first, what it contains, that it subsists for itself quite à *priori* and independent on empirical principles; and next in what it is distinguished from all other practical principles. With the *deduction*, that is, the justification of its objective and universal validity, and the discernment of the possibility of such a synthetical proposition à *priori*, we cannot expect to succeed so well as in the case of the principles of pure theoretical reason. For these referred to objects of possible experience, namely, to phenomena; and we could prove that these phenomena could be *known* as objects of experience only by being brought under the categories in accordance with these laws; and consequently that all possible experience must conform to these laws. But I could not proceed in this way with the deduction of the moral law. For this does not concern the knowledge of the properties of objects, which may be given to the reason from some other source; but a knowledge which can itself be the ground of the existence of the objects, and by which reason in a rational being has causality, *i.e.* pure reason, which can be regarded as a faculty immediately determining the will.

Now all our human insight is at an end as soon as we have arrived at fundamental powers or faculties; for the possibility of these cannot be understood by any means, and just as little should it be arbitrarily invented and assumed. Therefore, in the theoretic use of reason, it is experience alone that can justify us in assuming them. But this expedient of adducing empirical proofs, instead of a deduction from *à priori* sources of knowledge, is denied us here in respect to the pure practical faculty of reason. For whatever requires to draw the proof of its reality from experience must depend for the grounds of its possibility on principles of experience; and pure, yet practical, reason by its very notion cannot be regarded as such. Further, the moral law is given as a fact of pure reason of which we are *à priori* conscious, and which is apodictically certain, though it be granted that in experience no example of its exact fulfilment can be found. Hence the objective reality of the moral law cannot be proved by any deduction by any efforts of theoretical reason, whether speculative or empirically supported, and therefore, even if we renounced its apodictic certainty, it could not be proved *à posteriori* by experience, and yet it is firmly established of itself.

But instead of this vainly sought deduction of the moral principle, something else is found which was quite unexpected, namely, that this moral principle serves conversely as the principle of the deduction of an inscrutable faculty which no experience could prove, but of which speculative reason was compelled at least to assume the possibility (in order to find amongst its cosmological ideas the unconditioned in the chain of causality, so as not to contradict itself)—I mean the faculty of freedom. The moral law, which itself does not require a justification, proves not merely the possibility of freedom, but that it really belongs to beings who recognize this law as binding on themselves. The moral law is in fact a law of the causality of free agents, and therefore of the possibility of a supersensible system of nature, just as the metaphysical law of events in the world of sense was a law of causality of the sensible system of nature; and it therefore determines what speculative philosophy was compelled to leave undetermined, namely, the law for a causality, the concept of which in the latter was only negative; and therefore for the first time gives this concept objective reality.

This sort of credential of the moral law, viz. that it is set forth as a principle of the deduction of freedom, which is a causality of pure reason, is a sufficient substitute for all *à priori* justification, since theoretic reason was compelled to assume *at least* the possibility of freedom, in order to satisfy a want of its own. For the moral law proves its reality, so as even to satisfy the critique of the speculative reason, by the fact that it adds a positive definition to a causality previously conceived only negatively, the possibility of which was incomprehensible to speculative reason, which yet was compelled to suppose it. For it adds the notion of a reason that directly determines the will (by imposing on its maxims the condition of a universal legislative form); and thus it is able for the first time to give objective, though only practical, reality to reason, which always became transcendent when it sought to proceed speculatively with its ideas. It thus changes the *transcendent* use of reason into an *immanent*[8] use (so that reason is itself, by means of ideas, an efficient cause in the field of experience).

The determination of the causality of beings in the world of sense, as such, can never be unconditioned; and yet for every series of conditions there must be something unconditioned, and therefore there must be a causality which is determined wholly by itself. Hence, the idea of freedom as a faculty of absolute spontaneity was not found to be a want, but *as far as its possibility is concerned,* an analytic principle of pure speculative reason. But as it is absolutely impossible to find in experience any example in accordance with this idea, because amongst the causes of things as phenomena, it would be impossible to meet with any absolutely unconditioned determination of causality, we were only able to *defend our supposition* that a freely acting cause might be a being in the world of sense, in so far as it is considered in the other point of view as a *noumenon*, showing that there is no contradiction in regarding all its actions as subject to physical conditions so far as they are phenomena, and yet regarding its causality as physically unconditioned, in so far as the acting being belongs to the world of understanding,[9] and in thus making the concept of freedom the regulative principle of reason. By this principle I do not indeed learn what the object is to which that sort of causality is attributed; but I remove the difficulty; for, on the one side, in the explanation of events in the world, and consequently also of the actions of rational beings, I leave to the mechanism of physical necessity the right of ascending from conditioned to condition *ad infinitum,* while on the other side I keep open for speculative reason the place which for it is vacant, namely, the intelligible, in order to transfer the unconditioned thither. But I was not able to *verify* this *supposition*; that is, to change it into the *knowledge* of a being so acting, not even into the knowledge of the possibility of such a being. This vacant place is now filled by pure practical reason with a definite law of causality in an intelligible world (causality with freedom), namely, the moral law. Speculative reason does not hereby gain anything as regards its insight, but only as regards the *certainty* of its problematical notion of freedom, which here obtains *objective reality*, which, though only practical, is nevertheless undoubted. Even the notion of causality—the application, and consequently the signification, of which holds properly only in relation to phenomena, so as to connect them into experiences (as is shown by the critique of pure reason)—is not so enlarged as to extend its use beyond these limits. For if reason sought to do this, it would have to show how the logical relation of principle and consequence can be used synthetically in a different sort of intuition from the sensible; that is how a *causa noumenon* is possible. This it can never do; and, as practical reason, it does not even concern itself with it, since it only places the *determining principle* of causality of man as a sensible creature (which is given) in *pure reason* (which is therefore called practical); and therefore it employs the notion of cause, not in order to know objects, but to determine causality in relation to objects in general. It can abstract altogether from the application of this notion to objects with a view to theoretical knowledge (since this concept is always found *à priori* in the understanding, even independently on any intuition). Reason, then, employs it only for a practical purpose, and hence we can transfer the determining principle of the will into the intelligible order of things, admitting, at the same time, that we cannot understand how the notion of cause can determine the knowledge of these things. But reason must cognise causality with respect to the actions of the will in the sensible world in a definite manner; otherwise, practical reason could not really produce any action. But as to the notion which it forms of its own causality as noumenon, it need not determine it theoretically with a view to the cognition of its supersensible existence, so as to give it significance in this way. For it acquires significance apart from this, though only for practical use, namely, through the moral law. Theoretically viewed, it remains always a pure *à priori* concept of the understanding, which can be applied to objects whether they have been given sensibly or not, although in the latter case it has no definite theoretical significance or application, but is only a formal, though essential, conception of the understanding relating to an object in general. The significance which reason gives it through the moral law is merely practical, inasmuch as the idea of the law of causality (of the will) has itself causality, or is its determining principle.

II.—*Of the right that Pure Reason in its practical use has to an extension which is not possible to it in its speculative use*

We have in the moral principle set forth a law of causality, the determining principle of which is set above all the conditions of the sensible world; we have it conceived how the will, as belonging to the intelligible world, is determinable, and therefore we have its subject (man) not merely *conceived* as belonging to a world of pure understanding, and in this respect unknown (which the critique of speculative reason enabled us to do), but also *defined* as regards his causality by means of a law which cannot be reduced to any physical law of the sensible world; and therefore our knowledge is *extended* beyond the limits of that world—a pretension which the critique of the pure reason declared to be futile in all speculation. Now, how is the practical use of pure reason here to be reconciled with the theoretical, as to the determination of the limits of its faculty ?

David Hume, of whom we may say that he commenced the assault on the claims of pure reason, which made a thorough investigation of it necessary, argued thus: the notion of *cause* is a notion that involves the *necessity* of the connexion of the existence of different things, and that, in so far as they are different, so that, given A, I know that something quite distinct therefrom, namely B, must necessarily also exist. Now necessity can be attributed to a connexion, only in so far as it is known *à priori*; for experience would only enable us to know of such a connexion that it exists, not that it necessarily exists. Now, it is impossible, says he, to know *à priori* and as necessary the connexion between one thing and another (or between one attribute and another quite distinct) when they have not been given in experience. Therefore the notion of a cause is fictitious and delusive, and, to speak in the mildest way, is an illusion, only excusable inasmuch as the *custom* (a *subjective* necessity) of perceiving certain things, or their attributes as often associated in existence along with or in succession to one another, is insensibly taken for an objective necessity of supposing such a connexion in the objects themselves, and thus the notion of a cause has been acquired surreptitiously and not legitimately; nay, it can never be so acquired or authenticated, since it demands a connexion in itself vain, chimerical, and untenable in presence of reason, and to which no object can ever correspond. In this way was *empiricism* first introduced as the sole source of principles, as far as all knowledge of the existence of things is concerned (mathematics therefore remaining excepted); and with empiricism the most thorough scepticism, even with regard to the whole science of nature (as philosophy). For on such principles we can never conclude from given attributes of things as existing to a consequence (for this would require the notion of cause, which involves the necessity of such a connexion); we can only, guided by imagination, expect similar cases—an expectation which is never certain, however often it has been fulfilled. Of no event could we say: a certain thing *must* have preceded it, on which it *necessarily* followed; that is, it must have a cause; and, therefore, however frequent the cases we have known in which there was such an antecedent, so that a rule could be derived from them, yet we never could suppose it as always and necessarily so happening; we should, therefore, be obliged to leave its share to blind chance, with which all use of reason comes to an end; and this firmly establishes scepticism in reference to arguments ascending from effects to causes, and makes it impregnable.

Mathematics escaped well, so far, because *Hume* thought that its propositions were analytical; that is, proceeded from one property to another, by virtue of identity, and consequently according to the principle of contradiction. This, however, is not the case, since, on the contrary, they are synthetical; and although geometry, for example, has not to do with the existence of things, but only with their *à priori* properties in a possible intuition, yet it proceeds just as in the case of the causal notion, from one property (A) to another wholly distinct (B), as necessarily connected with the former. Nevertheless, mathematical science, so highly vaunted for its apodictic certainty, must at last fall under this *empiricism* for the same reason for which *Hume* put custom in the place of objective necessity in the notion of cause, and, in spite of all its pride, must consent to lower its bold pretension of claiming assent *à priori*, and depend for assent to the universality of its propositions on the kindness of observers, who, when called as witnesses, would surely not hesitate to admit that what the geometer propounds as a theorem they have always perceived to be the fact, and, consequently, although it be not necessarily true, yet they would permit us to expect it to be true in the future. In this manner *Hume's* empiricism leads inevitably to scepticism, even with regard to mathematics, and consequently in every scientific theoretical use of reason (for this belongs either to philosophy or mathematics). Whether with such a terrible overthrow of the chief branches of knowledge, common reason will escape better, and will not rather become irrecoverably involved in this destruction of all knowledge, so that from the same principles a *universal* scepticism should follow (affecting, indeed, only the learned), this I will leave everyone to judge for himself.

As regards my own labours in the critical examination of pure reason, which were occasioned by *Hume's* sceptical teaching, but went much further, and embraced the whole field of pure theoretical reason in its synthetic use, and, consequently, the field of what is called metaphysics in general; I proceeded in the following manner with respect to the doubts raised by the Scottish philosopher touching the notion of causality. If *Hume* took the objects of experience for *things in themselves* (as is almost always done), he was quite right in declaring the notion of cause to be a deception and false illusion; for as to things in themselves, and their attributes as such, it is impossible to see why because A is given, B, which is different, must necessarily be also given, and therefore he could by no means admit such an *à priori* knowledge of things in themselves. Still less could this acute writer allow an empirical origin of this concept, since this is directly contradictory to the necessity of connexion which constitutes the essence of the notion of causality; hence the notion was proscribed, and in its place was put custom in the observation of the course of perceptions.

It resulted, however, from my inquiries, that the objects with which we have to do in experience are by no means things in themselves, but merely phenomena; and that although in the case of things in themselves it is impossible to see how, if A is supposed, it should be contradictory that B, which is quite different from A, should not also be supposed (*i.e.* to see the necessity of the connexion between A as cause and B as effect); yet it can very well be conceived that, as phenomena, they may be necessarily connected *in one experience* in a certain way (*e.g.* with regard to time-relations); so that they could not be separated without contradicting that connexion, by means of which this experience is possible in which they are objects, and in which alone they are cognisable by us. And so it was found to be in fact; so that I was able not only to prove the objective reality of the concept of cause in regard to objects of experience, but also to *deduce* it as an *à priori* concept by reason of the necessity of the connexion it implied; that is, to show the possibility of its origin from pure understanding without any empirical sources; and thus, after removing the sources of empiricism, I was also able to overthrow the inevitable consequence of this namely, scepticism, first with regard to physical science, and then with regard to mathematics (in which empiricism has just the same grounds), both being sciences which have reference to objects of possible experience; herewith overthrowing the thorough doubt of whatever theoretic reason professes to discern.

But how is it with the application of this category of causality (and all the others; for without them there can be no knowledge of anything existing) to things which are not objects of possible experience, but lie beyond its bounds? For I was able to deduce the objective reality of these concepts only with regard to *objects of possible experience.* But even this very fact, that I have saved them, only in case I have proved that objects may by means of them be thought, though not determined *à priori*; this it is that gives them a place in the pure understanding, by which they are referred to objects in general (sensible or not sensible). If anything is still wanting, it is that which is the condition of the *application* of these categories, and especially that of causality, to objects, namely, intuition; for where this is not given, the application *with a view to theoretic knowledge of the object,* as a noumenon, is impossible; and therefore if anyone ventures on it, is (as in the critique of the pure reason) absolutely forbidden. Still, the objective reality of the concept (of causality) remains, and it can be used even of noumena, but without our being able in the least to define the concept theoretically so as to produce knowledge. For that this concept, even in reference to an object, contains nothing impossible, was shown by this, that even while applied to objects of sense, its seat was certainly fixed in the pure understanding; and although, when referred to things in themselves (which cannot be objects of experience), it is not capable of being determined so as to represent a *definite object* for the purpose of theoretic knowledge; yet for any other purpose (for instance, a practical) it might be capable of being determined so as to have such application. This could not be the case if, as *Hume* maintained, this concept of causality contained something absolutely impossible to be thought.

In order now to discover this condition of the application of the said concept to noumena, we need only recall why we are not content with its application to objects of experience, but desire also to apply it to things in themselves. It will appear, then, that it is not a theoretic but a practical purpose that makes this a necessity. In speculation, even if we were successful in it, we should not really gain anything in the knowledge of nature, or generally with regard to such objects as are given, but we should make a wide step from the sensibly conditioned (in which we have already enough to do to maintain ourselves, and to follow carefully the chain of causes) to the supersensible, in order to complete our knowledge of principles and to fix its limits: whereas there always remains an infinite chasm unfilled between those limits and what we know: and we should have hearkened to a vain curiosity rather than a solid desire of knowledge.

But, besides the relation in which the *understanding* stands to objects (in theoretical knowledge), it has also a relation to the faculty of desire, which is therefore called the will, and the pure will, inasmuch as pure understanding (in this case called reason) is practical through the mere conception of a law. The objective reality of a pure will, or, what is the same thing, of a pure practical reason, is given in the moral law *à priori*, as it were, by a fact, for so we may name a determination of the will which is inevitable, although it does not rest on empirical principles. Now, in the notion of a will the notion of causality is already contained, and hence the notion of a pure will contains that of a causality accompanied with freedom, that is, one which is not determinable by physical laws, and consequently is not capable of any empirical intuition in proof of its reality, but, nevertheless, completely justifies its objective reality *à priori* in the pure practical law; not, indeed (as is easily seen) for the purposes of the theoretical, but of the practical use of reason. Now, the notion of a being that has free will is the notion of a *causa noumenon*; and that this notion involves no contradiction we are already assured by the fact that, inasmuch as the concept of cause has arisen wholly from pure understanding, and has its objective reality assured by the Deduction, as it is moreover in its origin independent on any sensible conditions, it is, therefore, not restricted to phenomena (unless we wanted to make a definite theoretic use of it), but can be applied equally to things that are objects of the pure understanding. But, since this application cannot rest on any intuition (for intuition can only be sensible), therefore, *causa noumenon,* as regards the theoretic use of reason, although a possible and thinkable, is yet an empty notion. Now, I do not desire by means of this to *understand theoretically* the nature of a being, *in so far* as it has a *pure* will; it is enough for me to have thereby designated it as such, and hence to combine the notion of causality with that of freedom (and what is inseparable from it, the moral law, as its determining principle). Now, this right I certainly have by virtue of the pure, not-empirical origin of the notion of cause, since I do not consider myself entitled to make any use of it except in reference to the moral law which determines its reality, that is, only a practical use.

If, with *Hume,* I had denied to the notion of causality all objective reality in its [theoretic[10]] use, not merely with regard to things in themselves (the supersensible), but also with regard to the objects of the senses, it would have lost all significance, and being a theoretically impossible notion would have been declared to be quite useless; and since what is nothing cannot be made any use of, the practical use of a concept *theoretically null* would have been absurd. But, as it is, the concept of a causality free from empirical conditions, although empty (*i.e.* without any appropriate intuition), is yet theoretically possible, and refers to an indeterminate object; but in compensation significance is given to it in the moral law, and consequently in a practical sense. I have, indeed, no intuition which should determine its objective theoretic reality, but not the less it has a real application, which is exhibited *in concreto* in intentions or maxims; that is, it has a practical reality which can be specified, and this is sufficient to justify it even with a view to noumena.

Now, this objective reality of a pure concept of the understanding in the sphere of the supersensible, once brought in, gives an objective reality also to all the other categories although only so far as they stand in *necessary* connexion with the determining principle of the will (the moral law); a reality only of practical application, which has not the least effect in enlarging our theoretical knowledge of these objects, or the discernment of their nature by pure reason. So we shall find also in the sequel that these categories refer only to beings as *intelligences*, and in them only to the relation of *reason* to the *will*; consequently, always only to the *practical*, and beyond this cannot pretend to any knowledge of these things; and whatever other properties belonging to the theoretical representation of supersensible things may be brought into connexion with these categories, this is not to be reckoned as knowledge, but only as a right (in a practical point of view, however, it is a necessity) to admit and assume such beings, even in the case where we [conceive[11]] supersensible beings (*e.g.* God) according to analogy, that is, a purely rational relation, of which we make a practical use with reference to what is sensible; and thus the application to the supersensible solely in a practical point of view does not give pure theoretic reason the least encouragement to run riot into the transcendent.

CHAPTER II

OF THE CONCEPT OF AN OBJECT OF PURE PRACTICAL REASON

By a concept of the practical reason I understand the idea of an object as an effect possible to be produced through freedom. To be an object of practical knowledge, as such, signifies, therefore, only the relation of the will to the action by which the object or its opposite would be realized; and to decide whether something is an object of *pure* practical reason or not, is only to discern the possibility or impossibility of *willing* the action by which, if we had the required power (about which experience must decide), a certain object would be realized. If the object be taken as the determining principle of our desire, it must first be known whether it is *physically* possible by the free use of our powers, before we decide whether it is an object of practical reason or not. On the other hand, if the law can be considered *à priori* as the determining principle of the action, and the latter therefore as determined by pure practical reason; the judgment whether a thing is an object of pure practical reason or not does not depend at all on the comparison with our physical power; and the question is only whether we should *will* an action that is directed to the existence of an object, if the object were in our power; hence the previous question is only as to the *moral possibility* of the action, for in this case it is not the object, but the law of the will, that is the determining principle of the action. The only objects of practical reason are therefore those of *good* and *evil*. For by the former is meant an object necessarily desired according to a principle of reason; by the latter one necessarily shunned, also according to a principle of reason.

If the notion of good is not to be derived from an antecedent practical law, but, on the contrary, is to serve as its foundation, it can only be the notion of something whose existence promises pleasure, and thus determines the causality of the subject to produce it, that is to say, determines the faculty of desire. Now, since it is impossible to discern *à priori* what idea will be accompanied with *pleasure,* and what with *pain,* it will depend on experience alone to find out what is primarily[1] good or evil. The property of the subject, with reference to which alone this experiment can be made, is the *feeling* of pleasure and pain, a receptivity belonging to the internal sense; thus that only would be primarily good with which the sensation of *pleasure* is immediately connected, and that simply evil which immediately excites *pain.* Since, however, this is opposed even to the usage of language, which distinguishes the *pleasant* from the *good,* the *unpleasant* from the *evil,* and requires that good and evil shall always be judged by reason, and, therefore, by concepts which can be communicated to everyone, and not by mere sensation, which is limited to individual subjects[2] and their susceptibility; and, since nevertheless, pleasure or pain cannot be connected with any idea of an object *à priori,* the philosopher who thought himself obliged to make a feeling of pleasure the foundation of his practical judgments would call that *good* which is a *means* to the pleasant, and *evil,* what is a cause of unpleasantness and pain; for the judgment on the relation of means to ends certainly belongs to reason. But, although reason is alone capable of discerning the connexion of means with their ends (so that the will might even be defined as the faculty of ends, since these are always determining principles of the desires), yet the practical maxims which would follow from the aforesaid principle of the good being merely a means, would never contain as the object of the will anything good in itself, but only something good *for something*; the good would always be merely the useful, and that for which it is useful must always lie outside the will, in sensation. Now if this as a pleasant sensation were to be distinguished from the notion of good, then there would be nothing primarily good at all, but the good would have to be sought only in the means to something else, namely, some pleasantness.

It is an old formula of the schools: *Nihil appetimus nisi sub ratione boni; Nihil aversamur nisi sub ratione mali*; and it is used often correctly, but often also in a manner injurious to philosophy, because the expressions *boni* and *mali* are ambiguous, owing to the poverty of language, in consequence of which they admit a double sense, and, therefore, inevitably bring the practical laws into ambiguity; and philosophy, which in employing them becomes aware of the different meanings in the same word, but can find no special expressions for them, is driven to subtle distinctions about which there is subsequently no unanimity, because the distinction could not be directly marked by any suitable expression.[3]

The German language has the good fortune to possess expressions which do not allow this difference to be overlooked. It possesses two very distinct concepts, and especially distinct expressions, for that which the Latins express by a single word, *bonum*. For *bonum* it has "das Gute" [good], and "das Wohl" [well, weal], for *malum* "das Böse" [evil], and "das Übel" [ill, bad], or "das Weh" [woe]. So that we express two quite distinct judgments when we consider in an action the *good* and *evil* of it, or our *weal* and *woe* (ill). Hence it already follows that the above-quoted psychological proposition is at least very doubtful if it is translated: "we desire nothing except with a view to our *weal* or *woe*"; on the other hand, if we render it thus: "under the direction of reason we desire nothing except so far as we esteem it good or evil," it is indubitably certain, and at the same time quite clearly expressed.[4]

Well or *ill* always implies only a reference to our condition, as *pleasant* or *unpleasant*, as one of pleasure or pain, and if we desire or avoid an object on this account, it is only so far as it is referred to our sensibility and to the feeling of pleasure or pain that it produces. But *good* or *evil* always implies a reference to the *will*, as determined by the *law of reason* to make something its object; for it is never determined directly by the object and the idea of it, but is a faculty of taking a rule of reason for the motive of an action (by which an object may be realised). Good and evil, therefore, are properly referred to actions, not to the sensations of the person, and if anything is to be good or evil absolutely (*i.e.* in every respect and without any further condition), or is to be so esteemed, it can only be the manner of acting, the maxim of the will, and consequently the acting person himself as a good or evil man that can be so called, and not a thing.

However, then, men may laugh at the Stoic, who in the severest paroxysms of gout cried out: Pain, however thou tormentest me, I will never admit that thou art an evil (κακόν, *malum*): he was right. A bad thing it certainly was, and his cry betrayed that; but that any evil attached to him thereby, this he had no reason whatever to admit, for pain did not in the least diminish the worth of his person, but only that of his condition. If he had been conscious of a single lie, it would have lowered his pride, but pain served only to raise it, when he was conscious that he had not deserved it by any unrighteous action by which he had rendered himself worthy of punishment.

What we call good must be an object of desire in the judgment of every rational man, and evil an object of aversion in the eyes of everyone; therefore, in addition to sense, this judgment requires reason. So it is with truthfulness, as opposed to lying; so with justice, as opposed to violence, &c. But we may call a thing a bad [or ill] thing, which yet everyone must at the same time acknowledge to be good, sometimes directly, sometimes indirectly. The man who submits to a surgical operation feels it no doubt as a bad [ill] thing, but by their reason he and everyone acknowledge it to be good. If a man who delights in annoying and vexing peaceable people at last receives a right good beating, this is no doubt a bad [ill] thing; but everyone approves it and regards it as a good thing, even though nothing else resulted from it; nay, even the man who receives it must in his reason acknowledge that he has met justice, because he sees the proportion between good conduct and good fortune, which reason inevitably places before him, here put into practice.

No doubt our weal and woe are of *very great* importance in the estimation of our practical reason, and as far as our nature as sensible beings is concerned, our *happiness* is the only thing of *consequence*, provided it is estimated as reason especially requires, not by the transitory sensation, but by the influence that this has on our whole existence, and on our satisfaction therewith; but it is not *absolutely the only thing* of consequence. Man is a being who, as belonging to the world of sense, has wants, and so far his reason has an office which it cannot refuse, namely, to attend to the interest of his sensible nature, and to form practical maxims, even with a view to the happiness of this life, and if possible even to that of a future. But he is not so completely an animal as to be indifferent to what reason says on its own account, and to use it merely as an instrument for the satisfaction of his wants as a sensible being. For the possession of reason would not raise his worth above that of the brutes, if it is to serve him only for the same purpose that instinct serves in them; it would in that case be only a particular method which nature had employed to equip man for the same ends for which it has qualified brutes, without qualifying him for any higher purpose. No doubt once this arrangement of nature has been made for him, he requires reason in order to take into consideration his weal and woe; but besides this he possesses it for a higher purpose also, namely, not only to take into consideration what is good or evil in itself, about which only pure reason, uninfluenced by any sensible interest, can judge, but also to distinguish this estimate thoroughly from the former, and to make it the supreme condition thereof.

In estimating what is good or evil in itself, as distinguished from what can be so called only relatively, the following points are to be considered. Either a rational principle is already conceived as of itself the determining principle of the will, without regard to possible objects of desire (and therefore by the mere legislative form of the maxim), and in that case that principle is a practical *à priori* law, and pure reason is supposed to be practical of itself. The law in that case determines the will directly; the action conformed to it is *good in itself*; a will whose maxim always conforms to this law is *good absolutely in every respect,* and is the *supreme condition of all good.* Or the maxim of the will is consequent on a determining principle of desire which presupposes an object of pleasure or pain, something therefore that *pleases* or *displeases;* and the maxim of reason that we should pursue the former and avoid the latter determines our actions as good relatively to our inclination, that is, good indirectly (*i.e.* relatively to a different end to which they are means), and in that case these maxims can never be called laws, but may be called rational practical precepts. The end itself, the pleasure that we seek, is in the latter case not a *good* but a *welfare;* not a concept of reason, but an empirical concept of an object of sensation; but the use of the means thereto, that is, the action, is nevertheless called good (because rational deliberation is required for it), not, however, good absolutely, but only relatively to our sensuous nature, with regard to its feelings of pleasure and displeasure; but the will whose maxim is affected thereby is not a pure will; this is directed only to that in which pure reason by itself can be practical.

This is the proper place to explain the paradox of method in a critique of Practical Reason, namely, *that the concept of good and evil must not be determined before the moral law (of which it seems as if it must be the foundation), but only after it and by means of it.* In fact, even if we did not know that the principle of morality is a pure *à priori* law determining the will, yet, that we may not assume principles quite gratuitously, we must, at least at first, leave it *undecided,* whether the will has merely empirical principles of determination, or whether it has not also pure *à priori* principles; for it is contrary to all rules of philosophical method to assume as decided that which is the very point in question. Supposing that we wished to begin with the concept of good, in order to deduce from it the laws of the will, then this concept of an object (as a good) would at the same time assign to us this object as the sole determining principle of the will. Now, since this concept had not any practical *à priori* law for its standard, the criterion of good or evil could not be placed in anything but the agreement of the object with our feeling of pleasure or pain; and the use of reason could only consist in determining in the first place this pleasure or pain in connexion with all the sensations of my existence, and in the second place the means of securing to myself the object of the pleasure. Now, as experience alone can decide what conforms to the feeling of pleasure, and by hypothesis the practical law is to be based on this as a condition, it follows that the possibility of *à priori* practical laws would be at once excluded, because it was imagined to be necessary first of all to find an object the concept of which, as a good, should constitute the universal though empirical principle of determination of the will. But what it was necessary to inquire first of all was whether there is not an *à priori* determining principle of the will (and this could never be found anywhere but in a pure practical law, in so far as this law prescribes to maxims merely their form without regard to an object). Since, however, we laid the foundation of all practical law in an object determined by our conceptions of good and evil, whereas without a previous law that object could only be conceived by empirical concepts, we have deprived ourselves beforehand of the possibility of even conceiving a pure practical law. On the other hand, if we had first investigated the latter analytically, we should have found that it is not the concept of good as an object that determines the moral law, and makes it possible, but that, on the contrary, it is the moral law that first determines the concept of good, and makes it possible, so far as it deserves the name of good absolutely.

This remark, which only concerns the method of ultimate Ethical inquiries, is of importance. It explains at once the occasion of all the mistakes of philosophers with respect to the supreme principle of morals. For they sought for an object of the will which they could make the matter and principle of a law (which consequently could not determine the will directly but by means of that object referred to the feeling of pleasure or pain); whereas they ought first to have searched for a law that would determine the will *à priori* and directly, and afterwards determine the object in accordance with the will. Now, whether they placed this object of pleasure, which was to supply the supreme conception of goodness, in happiness, in perfection, in moral [feeling[5]], or in the will of God, their principle in every case implied heteronomy, and they must inevitably come upon empirical conditions of moral law since their object, which was to be the immediate principle of the will, could not be called good or bad except in its immediate relation to feeling, which is always empirical. It is only a formal law— that is, one which prescribes to reason nothing more than the form of its universal legislation as the supreme condition of its maxims—that can be *à priori* a determining principle of practical reason. The ancients avowed this error without concealment by directing all their moral inquiries to the determination of the notion of the *summum bonum*, which they intended afterwards to make the determining principle of the will in the moral law; whereas it is only far later, when the moral law has been first established for itself, and shown to be the direct determining principle of the will, that this object can be presented to the will, whose form is now determined *à priori*; and this we shall undertake in the Dialectic of the pure practical reason. The moderns, with whom the question of the *summum bonum* has gone out of fashion, or at least seems to have become a secondary matter, hide the same error under vague (expressions as in many other cases). It shows itself, nevertheless, in their systems, as it always produces heteronomy of practical reason; and from this can never be derived a moral law giving universal commands.

Now, since the notions of good and evil, as consequences of the *à priori* determination of the will, imply also a pure practical principle, and therefore a causality of pure reason; hence they do not originally refer to objects (so as to be, for instance, special modes of the synthetic unity of the manifold of given intuitions in one consciousness[6]) like the pure concepts of the understanding or categories of reason in its theoretic employment; on the contrary, they presuppose that objects, are given; but they are all modes (*modi*) of a single category, namely, that of causality, the determining principle of which consists in the rational conception of a law, which as a law of freedom reason gives to itself, thereby *à priori* proving itself practical. However, as the actions *on the one side* come under a law which is not a physical law, but a law of freedom, and consequently belong to the conduct of beings in the world of intelligence, yet on the *other side* as events in the world of sense they belong to phenomena; hence the determinations of a practical reason are only possible in reference to the latter, and therefore in accordance with the categories of the understanding; not indeed with a view to any theoretic employment of it, *i.e.* so as to bring the manifold of (sensible) *intuition* under one consciousness *à priori*; but only to subject the manifold of *desires* to the unity of consciousness of a practical reason, giving it commands in the moral law, *i.e.* to a pure will *à priori*.

These *categories of freedom*—for so we choose to call them in contrast to those theoretic categories which are categories of physical nature—have an obvious advantage over the latter, inasmuch as the latter are only forms of thought which designate objects in an indefinite manner by means of universal concepts for every possible intuition; the former, on the contrary, refer to the determination of a *free elective will* (to which indeed no exactly corresponding intuition can be assigned, but which has as its foundation a pure practical *à priori* law, which is not the case with any concepts belonging to the theoretic use of our cognitive faculties); hence, instead of the form of intuition (space and time), which does not lie in reason itself, but has to be drawn from another source, namely, the sensibility, these being elementary practical concepts have as their foundation the *form of a pure will*, which is given in reason, and therefore in the thinking faculty itself. From this it happens that as all precepts of pure practical reason have to do only with the *determination of the will*, not with the physical conditions (of practical ability) of the *execution of one's purpose*, the practical *à priori* principles in relation to the supreme principle of freedom are at once cognitions, and have not to wait for intuitions in order to acquire significance, and that for this remarkable reason, because they themselves produce the reality of that to which they refer (the intention of the will), which is not the case with theoretical concepts. Only we must be careful to observe that these categories only apply to the practical reason; and thus they proceed in order from those which are as yet subject to sensible conditions and morally indeterminate to those which are free from sensible conditions, and determined merely by the moral law.

*Table of the Categories of Freedom relatively to the
Notions of Good and Evil*

I.—QUANTITY

Subjective, according to maxims (*practical opinions* of the individual).
Objective, according to principles (*precepts*).
À priori, both objective and subjective principles of freedom (*laws*).

II.—QUALITY

Practical rules of *action* (*præceptivæ*).
Practical rules of *omission* (*prohibitivæ*).
Practical rules of *exception* (*exceptivæ*).

III.—RELATION

To *personality.*
To the *condition* of the person.
Reciprocal, of one person to the condition of the others.

IV.—MODALITY

The *permitted* and the *forbidden.*
Duty and the *contrary to duty.*
Perfect and *imperfect duty.*

It will at once be observed that in this table freedom is considered as a sort of causality not subject to empirical principles of determination, in regard to actions possible by it, which are phenomena in the world of sense, and that consequently it is referred to the categories which concern its physical possibility, whilst yet each category is taken so universally that the determining principle of that causality can be placed outside the world of sense in freedom as a property of a being in the world of intelligence; and finally the categories of modality introduce the transition from practical principles generally to those of morality, but only *problematically*. These can be established *dogmatically* only by the moral law.

I add nothing further here in explanation of the present table, since it is intelligible enough of itself. A division of this kind based on principles is very useful in any science, both for the sake of thoroughness and intelligibility. Thus, for instance, we know from the preceding table and its first number what we must begin from in practical inquiries, namely, from the maxims which everyone founds on his own inclinations; the precepts which hold for a species of rational beings so far as they agree in certain inclinations; and finally the law which holds for all without regard to their inclinations, &c. In this way we survey the whole plan of what has to be done, every question of practical philosophy that has to be answered, and also the order that is to be followed.

Of the Typic of the Pure Practical Judgment

It is the notions of good and evil that first determine an object of the will. They themselves, however, are subject to a practical rule of reason, which, if it is pure reason, determines the will *à priori* relatively to its object. Now, whether an action which is possible to us in the world of sense comes under the rule or not, is a question to be decided by the practical Judgment, by which what is said in the rule universally (*in abstracto*) is applied to an action *in concreto*. But since a practical rule of pure reason *in the first place* as *practical* concerns the existence of an object, and in *the second place* as a *practical rule* of pure reason implies necessity as regards the existence of the action, and therefore is a practical law, not a physical law depending on empirical principles of determination, but a law of freedom by which the will is to be determined independently on anything empirical (merely by the conception of a law and its form), whereas all instances that can occur of possible actions can only be empirical, that is, belong to the experience of physical nature; hence, it seems absurd to expect to find in the world of sense a case which, while as such it depends only on the law of nature, yet admits of the application to it of a law of freedom, and to which we can apply the supersensible idea of the morally good which is to be exhibited in it *in concreto*. Thus, the Judgment of the pure practical reason is subject to the same difficulties as that of the pure theoretical reason. The latter, however, had means at hand of escaping from these difficulties, because, in regard to the theoretical employment, intuitions were required to which pure concepts of the understanding could be applied, and such intuitions (though only of objects of the senses) can be given *à priori*, and therefore, as far as regards the union of the manifold in them, conforming to the pure *à priori* concepts of the understanding as *schemata*. On the other hand, the morally good is something whose object is supersensible; for which, therefore, nothing corresponding can be found in any sensible intuition. Judgment depending on laws of pure practical reason seems, therefore, to be subject to special difficulties arising from this, that a law of freedom is to be applied to actions, which are events taking place in the world of sense, and which, so far, belong to physical nature.

But here again is opened a favourable prospect for the pure practical Judgment. When I subsume under a *pure practical law* an action possible to me in the world of sense, I am not concerned with the possibility of the *action* as an event in the world of sense. This is a matter that belongs to the decision of reason in its theoretic use according to the law of causality, which is a pure concept of the understanding, for which reason has a *schema* in the sensible intuition. Physical causality, or the condition under which it takes place, belongs to the physical concepts, the schema of which is sketched by transcendental imagination. Here, however, we have to do, not with the schema of a case that occurs according to laws, but with the schema of a law itself (if the word is allowable here), since the fact that the will (not the action relatively to its effect) is determined by the law alone without any other principle, connects the notion of causality with quite different conditions from those which constitute physical connexion.

The physical law being a law to which the objects of sensible intuition, as such, are subject, must have a schema corresponding to it— that is, a general procedure of the imagination (by which it exhibits *à priori* to the senses the pure concept of the understanding which the law determines). But the law of freedom (that is, of a causality not subject to sensible conditions), and consequently the concept of the unconditionally good, cannot have any intuition, nor consequently any schema supplied to it for the purpose of its application *in concreto.* Consequently the moral law has no faculty but the understanding to aid its application to physical objects (not the imagination); and the understanding for the purposes of the judgment can provide for an idea of the reason, not a *schema* of the sensibility, but a law, though only as to its form as law; such a law, however, as can be exhibited *in concreto* in objects of the senses, and, therefore a law of nature. We can therefore call this law the *Type* of the moral law.

The rule of the judgment according to laws of pure practical reason is this: ask yourself whether, if the action you propose were to take place by a law of the system of nature of which you were yourself a part, you could regard it as possible by your own will. Everyone does, in fact, decide by this rule whether actions are morally good or evil. Thus, people say: If *everyone* permitted himself to deceive, when he thought it to his advantage; or thought himself justified in shortening his life as soon as he was thoroughly weary of it; or looked with perfect indifference on the necessity of others; and if you belonged to such an order of things, would you do so with the assent of your own will? Now everyone knows well that if he secretly allows himself to deceive, it does not follow that everyone else does so; or if, unobserved, he is destitute of compassion, others would not necessarily be so to him; hence, this comparison of the maxim of his actions with a universal law of nature is not the determining principle of his will. Such a law is, nevertheless, a *type* of the estimation of the maxim on moral principles. If the maxim of the action is not such as to stand the test of the form of a universal law of nature, then it is morally impossible. This is the judgment even of common sense; for its ordinary judgments, even those of experience, are always based on the law of nature. It has it, therefore, always at hand, only that in cases where *causality from freedom* is to be criticized, it makes that *law of nature* only the type of a *law of freedom*, because without something which it could use as an example in a case of experience, it could not give the law of a pure practical reason its proper use in practice.

It is therefore allowable to use the *system of the world of sense* as the *type* of a *supersensible system of things*, provided I do not transfer to the latter the intuitions, and what depends on them, but merely apply to it the *form* of *law* in general (the notion of which occurs even in the [commonest][7] use of reason, but cannot be definitely known *à priori* for any other purpose than the pure practical use of reason); for laws, as such, are so far identical, no matter from what they derive their determining principles.

Further, since of all the supersensible absolutely nothing [is known] except freedom (through the moral law), and this only so far as it is inseparably implied in that law, and moreover all supersensible objects to which reason might lead us, following the guidance of that law, have still no reality for us, except for the purpose of that law, and for the use of mere practical reason; and as reason is authorized and even compelled to use physical nature (in its pure form as an object of the understanding) as the type of the judgment; hence, the present remark will serve to guard against reckoning amongst concepts themselves that which belongs only to the *typic* of concepts. This, namely, as a typic of the judgment, guards against the *empiricism* of practical reason, which founds the practical notions of good and evil merely on experienced consequences (so-called happiness). No doubt happiness and the infinite advantages which would result from a will determined by self-love, if this will at the same time erected itself into a universal law of nature, may certainly serve as a perfectly suitable type for the morally good, but it is not identical with it. The same typic guards also against the *mysticism* of practical reason, which turns what served only as a *symbol* into a *schema*, that is, proposes to provide for the moral concepts actual intuitions, which, however, are not sensible (intuitions of an invisible Kingdom of God), and thus plunges into the transcendent. What is befitting the use of the moral concepts is only the *rationalism* of the judgment, which takes from the sensible system of nature only what pure reason can also conceive of itself, that is, conformity to law, and transfers into the supersensible nothing but what can conversely be actually exhibited by actions in the world of sense according to the formal rule of a law of nature. However, the caution against *empiricism* of practical reason is much more important; for[8] *mysticism* is quite reconcilable with the purity and sublimity of the moral law, and, besides, it is not very natural or agreeable to common habits of thought to strain one's imagination to supersensible intuitions; and hence the danger on this side is not so general. Empiricism, on the contrary, cuts up at the roots the morality of intentions (in which, and not in actions only, consists the high worth that men can and ought to give to themselves), and substitutes for duty something quite different, namely, an empirical interest, with which the inclinations generally are secretly leagued; and empiricism, moreover, being on this account allied with all the inclinations which (no matter what fashion they put on) degrade humanity when they are raised to the dignity of a supreme practical principle; and as these, nevertheless, are so favourable to everyone's feelings, it is for that reason much more dangerous than mysticism, which can never constitute a lasting condition of any great number of persons.

CHAPTER III

OF THE MOTIVES OF
PURE PRACTICAL REASON

WHAT is essential in the moral worth of actions is *that the moral law should directly determine the will.* If the determination of the will takes place in conformity indeed to the moral law, but only by means of a feeling, no matter of what kind, which has to be pre-supposed in order that the law may be sufficient to determine the will, and therefore not *for the sake of the law,* then the action will possess *legality* but not *morality,* Now, if we understand by *motive* [or *spring*] (*elater animi*) the subjective ground of determination of the will of a being whose reason does not necessarily conform to the objective law, by virtue of its own nature, then it will follow, first, that no motives can be attributed to the Divine will, and that the motives of the human will (as well as that of every created rational being) can never be anything else than the moral law, and conse-quently that the objective principle of determination must always and alone be also the subjectively sufficient determining principle of the action, if this is not merely to fulfil the *letter* of the law, with-out containing its *spirit.*[1]

Since, then, for the purpose of giving the moral law influence over the will, we must not seek for any other motives that might enable us to dispense with the motive of the law itself, because that would produce mere hypocrisy, without consistency; and it is even *dangerous* to allow other motives (for instance, that of interest) even to co-operate *along with* the moral law; hence nothing is left us but to determine carefully in what way the moral law becomes a motive, and what effect this has upon the faculty of desire. For as to the question how a law can be directly and of itself a determining principle of the will (which is the essence of morality), this is, for human reason, an insoluble problem and identical with the question: how a free will is possible. Therefore what we have to show *à priori* is, not why the moral law in itself supplies a motive, but what effect it, as such, produces (or, more correctly speaking, must produce) on the mind.

The essential point in every determination of the will by the moral law, is that being a free will it is determined simply by the moral law, not only without the co-operation of sensible impulses, but even to the rejection of all such, and to the checking of all inclinations so far as they might be opposed to that law. So far, then, the effect of the moral law as a motive is only negative, and this motive can be known *à priori* to be such. For all inclination and every sensible impulse is founded on feeling, and the negative effect produced on feeling (by the check on the inclinations) is itself feeling; consequently, we can see *à priori* that the moral law, as a determining principle of the will, must by thwarting all our inclinations produce a feeling which may be called pain; and in this we have the first, perhaps the only, instance in which we are able from *à priori* considerations to determine the relation of a cognition (in this case of pure practical reason) to the feeling of pleasure or displeasure. All the inclinations together (which can be reduced to a tolerable system, in which case their satisfaction is called happiness) constitute *self-regard* (*solipsismus*). This is either the *self-love* that consists in an excessive *fondness* for oneself (*philautia*), or satisfaction with oneself (*arrogantia*). The former is called particularly *selfishness*; the latter *self-conceit*. Pure practical reason only *checks* selfishness, looking on it as natural and active in us even prior to the moral law, so far as to limit it to the condition of agreement with this law, and then it is called *rational self-love*. But self-conceit reason *strikes down* altogether, since all claims to self-esteem which precede agreement with the moral law are vain and unjustifiable, for the certainty of a state of mind that coincides with this law is the first condition of personal worth (as we shall presently show more clearly), and prior to this conformity any pretension to worth is false and unlawful. Now the propensity to self-esteem is one of the inclinations which the moral law checks, inasmuch as that esteem rests only on morality. Therefore the moral law breaks down self-conceit. But as this law is something positive in itself, namely, the form of an intellectual causality, that is, of freedom, it must be an object of respect; for by opposing the subjective antagonism of the inclinations it *weakens* self-conceit; and since it even *breaks down*, that is, humiliates this conceit, it is an object of the highest respect, and consequently is the foundation of a positive feeling which is not of empirical origin, but is known *à priori*. Therefore respect for the moral law is a feeling which is produced by an intellectual cause, and this feeling is the only one that we know quite *à priori*, and the necessity of which we can perceive.

In the preceding chapter we have seen that everything that presents itself as an object of the will prior to the moral law is by that law itself, which is the supreme condition of practical reason, excluded from the determining principles of the will which we have called the unconditionally good; and that the mere practical form which consists in the adaptation of the maxims to universal legislation first determines what is good in itself and absolutely, and is the basis of the maxims of a pure will, which alone is good in every respect. However, we find that our nature as sensible beings is such that the matter of desire (objects of inclination, whether of hope or fear) first presents itself to us; and our pathologically affected self, although it is in its maxims quite unfit for universal legislation, yet, just as if it constituted our entire self, strives to put its pretensions forward first, and to have them acknowledged as the first and original. This propensity to make ourselves in the subjective determining principles of our choice serve as the objective determining principle of the will generally may be called *self-love*; and if this pretends to be legislative as an unconditional practical principle, it may be called *self-conceit*. Now the moral law, which alone is truly objective (namely, in every respect), entirely excludes the influence of self-love on the supreme practical principle, and indefinitely checks the self-conceit that prescribes the subjective conditions of the former as laws. Now whatever checks our self-conceit in our own judgment humiliates; therefore the moral law inevitably humbles every man when he compares with it the physical propensities of his nature. That, the idea of which as a *determining principle of our will* humbles us in our self-consciousness, awakes *respect* for itself, so far as it is itself positive, and a determining principle. Therefore the moral law is even subjectively a cause of respect. Now since everything that enters into self-love belongs to inclination, and all inclination rests on feelings, and consequently whatever checks all the feelings together in self-love has necessarily, by this very circumstance, an influence on feeling; hence we comprehend how it is possible to perceive *à priori* that the moral can produce an effect on feeling, in that it excludes the inclinations and the propensity to make them the supreme practical condition, *i.e.* self-love, from all participation in the supreme legislation. This effect is on one side merely *negative*, but on the other side, relatively to the restricting principle of pure practical reason, it is *positive*. No special kind of feeling need be assumed for this under the name of a practical or moral feeling as antecedent to the moral law, and serving as its foundation.

The negative effect on feeling (unpleasantness) is *pathological*, like every influence on feeling, and like every feeling generally. But as an effect of the consciousness of the moral law, and consequently in relation to a supersensible cause, namely, the subject of pure practical reason which is the supreme lawgiver, this feeling of a rational being affected by inclinations is called humiliation (intellectual self-depreciation); but with reference to the positive source of this humiliation, the law, it is respect for it. There is indeed no feeling for this law; but inasmuch as it removes the resistance out of the way, this removal of an obstacle is, in the judgment of reason, esteemed equivalent to a positive help to its causality. Therefore this feeling may also be called a feeling of respect for the moral law, and for both reasons together *a moral feeling.*

While the moral law, therefore, is a formal determining principle of action by practical pure reason, and is moreover a material though only objective determining principle of the objects of action as called good and evil, it is also a subjective determining principle, that is, a motive to this action, inasmuch as it has influence on the morality of the subject, and produces a feeling conducive to the influence of the law on the will. There is here in the subject no *antecedent* feeling tending to morality. For this is impossible, since every feeling is sensible, and the motive of moral intention must be free from all sensible conditions. On the contrary, while the sensible feeling which is at the bottom of all our inclinations is the condition of that impression which we call respect, the cause that determines it lies in the pure practical reason; and this impression therefore, on account of its origin, must be called, not a pathological but a *practical effect.* For by the fact that the conception of the moral law deprives self-love of its influence, and self-conceit of its illusion, it lessens the obstacle to pure practical reason, and produces the conception of the superiority of its objective law to the impulses of the sensibility; and thus, by removing the counterpoise, it gives relatively greater weight to the law in the judgment of reason (in the case of a will affected by the aforesaid impulses). Thus the respect for the law is not a motive to morality, but is morality itself subjectively considered as a motive, inasmuch as pure practical reason, by rejecting all the rival pretensions of self-love, gives authority to the law which now alone has influence. Now it is to be observed that as respect is an effect on feeling, and therefore on the sensibility, of a rational being, it presupposes this sensibility, and therefore also the finiteness of such beings on whom the moral law imposes respect; and that respect for the *law* cannot be attributed to a supreme being, or to any being free from all sensibility, in whom, therefore, this sensibility cannot be an obstacle to practical reason.

This feeling [sentiment] (which we call the moral feeling) is therefore produced simply by reason. It does not serve for the estimation of actions nor for the foundation of the objective moral law itself, but merely as a motive to make this of itself a maxim. But what name could we more suitably apply to this singular feeling which cannot be compared to any pathological feeling? It is of such a peculiar kind that it seems to be at the disposal of reason only, and that pure practical reason.

Respect applies always to persons only—not to things. The latter may arouse inclination, and if they are animals (*e.g.* horses, dogs, &c.), even *love* or *fear*, like the sea, a volcano, a beast of prey; but never *respect*. Something that comes nearer to this feeling is *admiration*, and this, as an affection, astonishment, can apply to things also, *e.g.* lofty mountains, the magnitude, number, and distance of the heavenly bodies, the strength and swiftness of many animals, &c. But all this is not respect. A man also may be an object to me of love, fear, or admiration, even to astonishment, and yet not be an object of respect. His jocose humour, his courage and strength, his power from the rank he has amongst others, may inspire me with sentiments of this kind, but still inner respect for him is wanting. *Fontenelle* says, "I bow before a great man, but my mind does not bow." I would add, before an humble plain man, in whom I perceive uprightness of character in a higher degree than I am conscious of in myself, *my mind bows* whether I choose it or not, and though I bear my head never so high that he may not forget my superior rank. Why is this? Because his example exhibits to me a law that humbles my self-conceit when I compare it with my conduct: a law, the *practicability* of obedience to which I see proved by fact before my eyes. Now, I may even be conscious of a like degree of uprightness, and yet the respect remains. For since in man all good is defective, the law made visible by an example still humbles my pride, my standard being furnished by a man whose imperfections, whatever they may be, are not known to me as my own are, and who therefore appears to me in a more favourable light. *Respect* is a *tribute* which we cannot refuse to merit, whether we will or not; we may indeed outwardly withhold it, but we cannot help feeling it inwardly.

Respect is so *far from being* a feeling of pleasure that we only reluctantly give way to it as regards a man. We try to find out something that may lighten the burden of it, some fault to compensate us for the humiliation which such an example causes. Even the dead are not always secure from this criticism, especially if their example appears inimitable. Even the moral law itself in its *solemn majesty* is exposed to this endeavour to save oneself from yielding it respect. Can it be thought that it is for any other reason that we are so ready to reduce it to the level of our familiar inclination, or that it is for any other reason that we all take such trouble to make it out to be the chosen precept of our own interest well understood, but that we want to be free from the deterrent respect which shows us our own unworthiness with such severity? Nevertheless, on the other hand, so *little* is there *pain* in it that if once one has laid aside self-conceit and allowed practical influence to that respect, he can never be satisfied with contemplating the majesty of this law, and the soul believes itself elevated in proportion as it sees the holy law elevated above it and its frail nature. No doubt great talents and activity proportioned to them may also occasion respect or an analogous feeling. It is very proper to yield it to them, and then it appears as if this sentiment were the same thing as admiration. But if we look closer, we shall observe that it is always uncertain how much of the ability is due to native talent, and how much to diligence in cultivating it. Reason represents it to us as probably the fruit of cultivation, and therefore as meritorious, and this notably reduces our self-conceit, and either casts a reproach on us or urges us to follow such an example in the way that is suitable to us. This respect, then, which we show to such a person (properly speaking, to the law that his example exhibits) is not mere admiration; and this is confirmed also by the fact, that when the common run of admirers think they have learned from any source the badness of such a man's character (for instance,

Voltaire's), they give up all respect for him; whereas the true scholar still feels it at least with regard to his talents, because he is himself engaged in a business and a vocation which make imitation of such a man in some degree a law.

Respect for the moral law is therefore the only and the undoubted moral motive, and this feeling is directed to no object, except on the ground of this law. The moral law first determines the will objectively and directly in the judgment of reason; and freedom, whose causality can be determined only by the law, consists just in this, that it restricts all inclinations, and consequently self-esteem, by the condition of obedience to its pure law. This restriction now has an effect on feeling, and produces the impression of displeasure which can be known *à priori* from the moral law. Since it is so far only a *negative* effect which, arising from the influence of pure practical reason, checks the activity of the subject, so far as it is determined by inclinations, and hence checks the opinion of his personal worth (which, in the absence of agreement with the moral law, is reduced to nothing); hence, the effect of this law on feeling is merely humiliation. We can, therefore, perceive this *à priori*, but cannot know by it the force of the pure practical law as a motive, but only the resistance to motives of the sensibility. But since the same law is objectively, that is, in the conception of pure reason, an immediate principle of determination of the will, and consequently this humiliation takes place only relatively to the purity of the law; hence, the lowering of the pretensions of moral self-esteem, that is, humiliation on the sensible side, is an elevation of the moral, *i.e.* practical, esteem for the law itself on the intellectual side; in a word, it is respect for the law, and therefore, as its cause is intellectual, a positive feeling which can be known *à priori*. For whatever diminishes the obstacles to an activity furthers this activity itself. Now the recognition of the moral law is the consciousness of an activity of practical reason from objective principles, which only fails to reveal its effect in actions because subjective (pathological) causes hinder it. Respect for the moral law, then, must be regarded as a positive, though indirect, effect of it on feeling, inasmuch as this respect[2] weakens the impeding influence of inclinations by humiliating self-esteem; and hence also as a subjective principle of activity, that is, as a *motive* to obedience to the law, and as a principle of the maxims of a life conformable to it. From the notion of a motive arises that of an *interest*, which can never be attributed to any being unless it possesses reason, and which signifies a *motive* of the will in so far as it is conceived by the reason. Since in a morally good will the law itself must be the motive, the *moral interest* is a pure interest of practical reason alone, independent on sense. On the notion of an interest is based that of a *maxim*. This, therefore, is morally good only in case it rests simply on the interest taken in obedience to the law. All three notions, however, that of a *motive*, of an *interest*, and of a *maxim*, can be applied only to finite beings. For they all suppose a limitation of the nature of the being, in that the subjective character of his choice does not of itself agree with the objective law of a practical reason; they suppose that the being requires to be impelled to action by something, because an internal obstacle opposes itself. Therefore they cannot be applied to the Divine will.

There is something so singular in the unbounded esteem for the pure moral law, apart from all advantage, as it is presented for our obedience by practical reason, the voice of which makes even the boldest sinner tremble, and compels him to hide himself from it, that we cannot wonder if we find this influence of a mere intellectual idea on the feelings quite incomprehensible to speculative reason, and have to be satisfied with seeing so much of this *à priori*, that such a feeling is inseparably connected with the conception of the moral law in every finite rational being. If this feeling of respect were pathological, and therefore were a feeling of pleasure based on the inner *sense*, it would be in vain to try to discover a connexion of it with any idea *à priori*. But [it[3]] is a feeling that applies merely to what is practical, and depends on the conception of a law, simply as to its form, not on account of any object, and therefore cannot be reckoned either as pleasure or pain, and yet produces an *interest* in obedience to the law, which we call the *moral interest*, just as the capacity of taking such an interest in the law (or respect for the moral law itself) is properly the *moral feeling* [or *sentiment*].

The consciousness of a *free* submission of the will to the law, yet combined with an inevitable constraint put upon all inclinations, though only by our own reason, is respect for the law. The law that demands this respect and inspires it is clearly no other than the moral (for no other precludes all inclinations from exercising any direct influence on the will). An action which is objectively practical according to this law, to the exclusion of every determining principle of inclination, is *duty*, and this by reason of that exclusion includes in its concept practical *obligation*, that is, a determination to actions, however *reluctantly* they may be done. The feeling that arises from the consciousness of this obligation is not pathological, as would be a feeling produced by an object of the senses, but practical only, that is, it is made possible by a preceding (objective) determination of the will and causality of the reason. As *submission* to the law, therefore, that is, as a command (announcing constraint for the sensibly affected subject), it contains in it no pleasure, but on the contrary, so far, pain in the action. On the other hand, however, as this constraint is exercised merely by the legislation of our *own* reason, it also contains something *elevating*, and this subjective effect on feeling, inasmuch as pure practical reason is the sole cause of it, may be called in this respect *self-approbation*, since we recognize ourselves as determined thereto solely by the law without any interest, and are now conscious of a quite different interest subjectively produced thereby, and which is purely practical and *free*; and our taking this interest in an action of duty is not suggested by any inclination, but is commanded and actually brought about by reason through the practical law; whence this feeling obtains a special name, that of respect.

The notion of duty, therefore, requires in the action, *objectively*, agreement with the law, and, subjectively in its maxim, that respect for the law shall be the sole mode in which the will is determined thereby. And on this rests the distinction between the consciousness of having acted *according to duty* and *from duty*, that is, from respect for the law. The former (*legality*) is possible even if inclinations have been the determining principles of the will; but the latter (*morality*), moral worth, can be placed only in this, that the action is done from duty, that is, simply for the sake of the law.[4]

It is of the greatest importance to attend with the utmost exactness in all moral judgments to the subjective principle of all maxims, that all the morality of actions may be placed in the necessity of acting *from duty* and from respect for the law, not from love and inclination for that which the actions are to produce. For men and all created rational beings moral necessity is constraint, that is obligation, and every action based on it is to be conceived as a duty, not as a proceeding previously pleasing, or likely to be pleasing to us of our own accord. As if indeed we could ever bring it about that without respect for the law, which implies fear, or at least apprehension of transgression, we of ourselves, like the independent Deity, could ever come into possession of *holiness* of will by the coincidence of our will with the pure moral law becoming as it were part of our nature, never to be shaken (in which case the law would cease to be a command for us, as we could never be tempted to be untrue to it).

The moral law is in fact for the will of a perfect being a law of *holiness*, but for the will of every finite rational being a law of *duty*, of moral constraint, and of the determination of its actions by *respect* for this law and reverence for its duty. No other subjective principle must be assumed as a motive, else while the action might chance to be such as the law prescribes, yet as it does not proceed from duty, the intention, which is the thing properly in question in this legislation, is not moral.

It is a very beautiful thing to do good to men from love to them and from sympathetic good will, or to be just from love of order; but this is not yet the true moral maxim of our conduct which is suitable to our position amongst rational beings as *men*, when we pretend with fanciful pride to set ourselves above the thought of duty, like volunteers, and, as if we were independent on the command, to want to do of our own good pleasure what we think we need no command to do. We stand under a *discipline* of reason, and in all our maxims must not forget our subjection to it, nor withdraw anything therefrom, or by an egotistic presumption diminish aught of the authority of the law (although our own reason gives it) so as to set the determining principle of our will, even though the law be conformed to, anywhere else but in the law itself and in respect for this law. Duty and obligation are the only names that we must give to our relation to the moral law. We are indeed legislative members of a moral kingdom rendered possible by freedom, and presented to us by reason as an object of respect; but yet we are subjects in it, not the sovereign, and to mistake our inferior position as creatures, and presumptuously to reject the authority of the moral law, is already to revolt from it in spirit, even though the letter of it is fulfilled.

With this agrees very well the possibility of such a command as: *Love God above everything, and thy neighbour as thyself.*[5] For as a command it requires respect for a law which *commands* love and does not leave it to our own arbitrary choice to make this our principle. Love to God, however, considered as an inclination (pathological love), is impossible, for he is not an object of the senses. The same affection towards men is possible no doubt, but cannot be commanded, for it is not in the power of any man to love anyone at command; therefore it is only *practical love* that is meant in that pith of all laws. To love God means, in this sense, to like to do His commandments; to love one's neighbour means to like to practise all duties towards him. But the command that makes this a rule cannot command us to *have* this disposition in actions conformed to duty, but only to *endeavour* after it. For a command to like to do a thing is in itself contradictory, because if we already know of ourselves what we are bound to do, and if further we are conscious of liking to do it, a command would be quite needless; and if we do it not willingly, but only out of respect for the law, a command that makes this respect the motive of our maxim would directly counteract the disposition commanded. That law of all laws, therefore, like all the moral precepts of the Gospel, exhibits the moral disposition in all its perfection, in which, viewed as an Ideal of holiness, it is not attainable by any creature, but yet is the pattern which we should strive to approach, and in an uninterrupted but infinite progress become like to. In fact, if a rational creature could ever reach this point, that he thoroughly *likes* to do all moral laws, this would mean that there does not exist in him even the possibility of a desire that would tempt him to deviate from them; for to overcome such a desire always costs the subject some sacrifice, and therefore requires self-compulsion, that is, inward constraint to something that one does not quite like to do; and no creature can ever reach this stage of moral disposition. For, being a creature, and therefore always dependent with respect to what he requires for complete satisfaction, he can never be quite free from desires and inclinations, and as these rest on physical causes, they can never of themselves coincide with the moral law,[6] the sources of which are quite different; and therefore they make it necessary to found the mental disposition of one's maxims on moral obligation, not on ready inclination, but on respect, which *demands* obedience to the law, even though one may not like it; not on love, which apprehends no inward reluctance of the will towards the law. Nevertheless, this latter, namely, love to the law (which would then cease to be a *command,* and then morality, which would have passed subjectively into holiness, would cease to be *virtue),* must be the constant though unattainable goal of his endeavours. For in the case of what we highly esteem, but yet (on account of the consciousness of our weakness) dread, the increased facility of satisfying it changes the most reverential awe into inclination, and respect into love: at least this would be the perfection of a disposition devoted to the law, if it were possible for a creature to attain it.[7]

This reflection is intended not so much to clear up the evangelical command just cited, in order to prevent *religious fanaticism* in regard to love of God, but to define accurately the moral disposition with regard directly to our duties towards men, and to check, or if possible prevent, *a merely moral fanaticism* which infects many persons. The stage of morality on which man (and, as far as we can see, every rational creature) stands is respect for the moral law. The disposition that he ought to have in obeying this is to obey it from duty, not from spontaneous inclination, or from an endeavour taken up from liking and unbidden; and this proper moral condition in which he can always be is *virtue*, that is, moral disposition *militant*, and not *holiness* in the fancied *possession* of a perfect *purity* of the disposition of the will. It is nothing but moral fanaticism and exaggerated self-conceit that is infused into the mind by exhortation to actions as noble, sublime, and magnani-mous, by which men are led into the delusion that it is not duty, that is, respect for the law, whose yoke (an easy yoke indeed, because reason itself imposes it on us) they *must* bear, whether they like it or not, that constitutes the determining principle of their actions, and which always humbles them while they *obey* it; fancying that those actions are expected from them, not from duty, but as pure merit. For not only would they, in imitating such deeds from such a principle, not have fulfilled the spirit of the law in the least, which consists not in the legality of the action (with-out regard to principle), but in the subjection of the mind to the law; not only do they make the motives *pathological* (seated in sym-pathy or self-love), not moral (in the law), but they produce in this way a vain, high-flying, fantastic way of thinking, flattering them-selves with a spontaneous goodness of heart that needs neither spur nor bridle, for which no command is needed, and thereby forgetting their obligation, which they ought to think of rather than merit. Indeed actions of others which are done with great sacrifice, and merely for the sake of duty, may be praised as *noble* and *sublime*, but only so far as there are traces which suggest that they were done wholly out of respect for duty and not from excited feelings. If these, however, are set before anyone as exam-ples to be imitated, respect for duty (which is the only true moral feeling) must be employed as the motive—this severe holy precept which never allows our vain self-love to dally with pathological impulses (however analogous they may be to morality), and to take a pride in *meritorious* worth. Now if we search we shall find for all actions that are worthy of praise a law of duty which *commands*, and does not leave us to choose what may be agreeable to our inclinations. This is the only way of representing things that can give a moral training to the soul, because it alone is capable of solid and accurately defined principles.

If *fanaticism* in its most general sense is a deliberate overstepping of the limits of human reason, then *moral fanaticism* is such an overstepping of the bounds that practical pure reason sets to mankind, in that it forbids us to place the subjective determining principle of correct actions, that is, their moral *motive*, in anything but the law itself, or to place the disposition which is thereby brought into the maxims in anything but respect for this law, and hence commands us to take as the supreme *vital principle* of all morality in men the thought of duty, which strikes down all *arrogance* as well as vain *self-love*.

If this is so, it is not only writers of romance or sentimental educators (although they may be zealous opponents of sentimentalism), but sometimes even philosophers, nay, even the severest of all, the Stoics, that have brought in *moral fanaticism* instead of a sober but wise moral discipline, although the fanaticism of the latter was more heroic, that of the former of an insipid, effeminate character; and we may, without hypocrisy, say of the moral teaching of the Gospel, that it first, by the purity of its moral principle, and at the same time by its suitability to the limitations of finite beings, brought all the good conduct of men under the discipline of a duty plainly set before their eyes, which does not permit them to indulge in dreams of imaginary moral perfections; and that it also set the bounds of humility (that is, self-knowledge) to self-conceit as well as to self-love, both which are ready to mistake their limits.

Duty! Thou sublime and mighty name that dost embrace nothing charming or insinuating, but requirest submission, and yet seekest not to move the will by threatening aught that would arouse natural aversion or terror, but merely holdest forth a law which of itself finds entrance into the mind, and yet gains reluctant reverence (though not always obedience), a law before which all inclinations are dumb, even though they secretly counter-work it; what origin is there worthy of thee, and where is to be found the root of thy noble descent which proudly rejects all kindred with the inclinations; a root to be derived from which is the indispensable condition of the only worth which men can give themselves?

It can be nothing less than a power which elevates man above himself (as a part of the world of sense), a power which connects him with an order of things that only the understanding can conceive, with a world which at the same time commands the whole sensible world, and with it the empirically determinable existence of man in time, as well as the sum-total of all ends (which totality alone suits such unconditional practical laws as the moral). This power is nothing but *personality*, that is, freedom and independence on the mechanism of nature, yet, regarded also as a faculty of a being which is subject to special laws, namely, pure practical laws given by its own reason; so that the person as belonging to the sensible world is subject to his own personality as belonging to the intelligible [supersensible] world. It is, then, not to be wondered at that man, as belonging to both worlds, must regard his own nature in reference to its second and highest characteristic only with reverence, and its laws with the highest respect.

On this origin are founded many expressions which designate the worth of objects according to moral ideas. The moral law is *holy* (inviolable). Man is indeed unholy enough; but he must regard *humanity* in his own person as holy. In all creation everything one chooses, and over which one has any power, may be used *merely as means*; man alone, and with him every rational creature, is an *end in himself.* By virtue of the autonomy of his freedom he is the subject of the moral law, which is holy. Just for this reason every will, even every person's own individual will, in relation to itself, is restricted to the condition of agreement with the *autonomy* of the rational being, that is to say, that it is not to be subject to any purpose which cannot accord with a law which might arise from the will of the passive subject himself; the latter is, therefore, never to be employed merely as means, but as itself also, concurrently, an end. We justly attribute this condition even to the Divine will, with regard to the rational beings in the world, which are His creatures, since it rests on their *personality*, by which alone they are ends in themselves.

This respect-inspiring idea of personality which sets before our eyes the sublimity of our nature (in its higher aspect), while at the same time it shows us the want of accord of our conduct with it, and thereby strikes down self-conceit, is even natural to the commonest reason, and easily observed. Has not every even moderately honourable man sometimes found that, where by an otherwise inoffensive lie he might either have withdrawn himself from an unpleasant business, or even have procured some advantage for a loved and well-deserving friend, he has avoided it solely lest he should despise himself secretly in his own eyes? When an upright man is in the greatest distress, which he might have avoided if he could only have disregarded duty, is he not sustained by the consciousness that he has maintained humanity in its proper dignity in his own person and honoured it, that he has no reason to be ashamed of himself in his own sight, or to dread the inward glance of self-examination? This consolation is not happiness, it is not even the smallest part of it, for no one would wish to have occasion for it, or would perhaps even desire a life in such circumstances. But he lives, and he cannot endure that he should be in his own eyes unworthy of life. This inward peace is therefore merely negative as regards what can make life pleasant; it is, in fact, only the escaping the danger of sinking in personal worth, after everything else that is valuable has been lost. It is the effect of a respect for something quite different from life, something in comparison and contrast with which life with all its enjoyment has no value. He still lives only because it is his duty, not because be finds anything pleasant in life.

Such is the nature of the true motive of pure practical reason; it is no other than the pure moral law itself, inasmuch as it makes us conscious of the sublimity of our own supersensible existence, and subjectively produces respect for their higher nature in men who are also conscious of their sensible existence and of the consequent dependence of their pathologically very susceptible nature. Now with this motive may be combined so many charms and satisfactions of life, that even on this account alone the most prudent choice of a rational *Epicurean* reflecting on the greatest advantage of life would declare itself on the side of moral conduct, and it may even be advisable to join this prospect of a cheerful enjoyment of life with that supreme motive which is already sufficient of itself; but only as a counterpoise to the attractions which vice does not fail to exhibit on the opposite side, and not so as, even in the smallest degree, to place in this the proper moving power when duty is in question. For that would be just the same as to wish to taint the purity of the moral disposition in its source. The majesty of duty has nothing to do with enjoyment of life; it has its special law and its special tribunal, and though the two should be never so well shaken together to be given well mixed, like medicine, to the sick soul, yet they will soon separate of themselves; and if they do not, the former will not act; and although physical life might gain somewhat in force, the moral life would fade away irrecoverably.

CRITICAL EXAMINATION OF THE ANALYTIC
OF PURE PRACTICAL REASON

By the critical examination of a science, or of a portion of it, which constitutes a system by itself, I understand the inquiry and proof why it must have this and no other systematic form, when we compare it with another system which is based on a similar faculty of knowledge. Now practical and speculative reason are based on the same faculty, so far as both are *pure reason*. Therefore the difference in their systematic form must be determined by the comparison of both, and the ground of this must be assigned.

The Analytic of pure theoretic reason had to do with the knowledge of such objects as may have been given to the understanding, and was obliged therefore to begin from *intuition*, and consequently (as this is always sensible) from sensibility; and only after that could advance to concepts (of the objects of this intuition), and could only end with *principles* after both these had preceded. On the contrary, since practical reason has not to do with objects so as to *know* them, but with its own faculty of *realizing* them (in accordance with the knowledge of them), that is, with a will which is a causality, inasmuch as reason contains its determining principle; since consequently it has not to furnish an object of intuition, but as practical reason has to furnish only a law (because the notion of causality always inplies the reference to a law which determines the existence of the many in relation to one another); hence a critical examination of the Analytic of reason, if this is to be practical reason (and this is properly the problem), must begin with the *possibility of practical principles à priori*. Only after that can it proceed to *concepts* of the objects of a practical reason, namely, those of absolute good and evil, in order to assign them in accordance with those principles (for prior to those principles they cannot possibly be given as good and evil by any faculty of knowledge), and only then could the section be concluded with the last chapter, that, namely, which treats of the relation of the pure practical reason to the sensibility and of its necessary influence thereon, which is *à priori* cognisable, that is, of the *moral sentiment*. Thus the Analytic of the practical pure reason has the whole extent of the conditions of its use in common with the theoretical, but in reverse order. The Analytic of pure theoretic reason was divided into transcendental Æsthetic and transcendental Logic, that of the practical reversely into Logic and Æsthetic of pure practical reason (if I may, for the sake of analogy merely, use these designations, which are not quite suitable). This logic again was there divided into the Analytic of concepts and that of principles: here into that of principles and concepts. The Æsthetic also had in the former cases two parts, on account of the two kinds of sensible intuition; here the sensibility is not considered as a capacity of intuition at all, but merely as feeling (which can be a subjective ground of desire), and in regard to it pure practical reason admits no further division.

It is also easy to see the reason why this division into two parts with its subdivision was not actually adopted here (as one might have been induced to attempt by the example of the former critique). For since it is *pure reason* that is here considered in its practical use, and consequently as proceeding from *à priori* principles, and not from empirical principles of determination, hence the division of the analytic of pure practical reason must resemble that of a syllogism, namely, proceeding from the universal in the *major premiss* (the moral principle), through a *minor premiss* containing a subsumption of possible actions (as good or evil) under the former, to the *conclusion*, namely, the subjective determination of the will (an interest in the possible practical good, and in the maxim founded on it). He who has been able to convince himself of the truth of the positions occurring in the Analytic will take pleasure in such comparisons; for they justly suggest the expectation that we may perhaps some day be able to discern the unity of the whole faculty of reason (theoretical as well as practical), and be able to derive all from one principle, which is what human reason inevitably demands, as it finds complete satisfaction only in a perfectly systematic unity of its knowledge.

If now we consider also the contents of the knowledge that we can have of a pure practical reason, and by means of it, as shown by the Analytic, we find, along with a remarkable analogy between it and the theoretical, no less remarkable differences. As regards the theoretical, the *faculty of a pure rational cognition à priori* could be easily and evidently proved by examples from sciences (in which, as they put their principles to the test in so many ways by methodical use, there is not so much reason as in common knowledge to fear a secret mixture of empirical principles of cognition). But, that pure reason without the admixture of any empirical principle is practical of itself, this could only be shown from the *commonest practical use of reason*, by verifying the fact, that every man's natural reason acknowledges the supreme practical principle as the supreme law of his will—a law completely *à priori*, and not depending on any sensible data. It was necessary first to establish and verify the purity of its origin, even in the *judgment of this common reason*, before science could take it in hand to make use of it, as a fact, that is, prior to all disputation about its possibility, and all the consequences that may be drawn from it. But this circumstance may be readily explained from what has just been said; because practical pure reason must necessarily begin with principles, which therefore must be the first data, the foundation of all science, and cannot be derived from it. It was possible to effect this verification of moral principles as principles of a pure reason quite well, and with sufficient certainty, by a single appeal to the judgment of common sense, for this reason, that anything empirical which might slip into our maxims as a determining principle of the will can be detected at once by the feeling of pleasure or pain which necessarily attaches to it as exciting desire; whereas pure practical reason positively *refuses* to admit this feeling into its principle as a condition. The heterogeneity of the determining principles (the empirical and rational) is clearly detected by this resistance of a practically legislating reason against every admixture of inclination, and by a peculiar kind of *sentiment*, which, however, does not precede the legislation of the practical reason, but, on the contrary, is produced by this as a constraint, namely, by the feeling of a respect such as no man has for inclinations of whatever kind but for the law only; and it is detected in so marked and prominent a manner that even the most uninstructed cannot fail to see at once in an example presented to him, that empirical principles of volition may indeed urge him to follow their attractions, but that he can never be expected to *obey* anything but the pure practical law of reason alone.

The distinction between the *doctrine of happiness* and the *doctrine of morality* [*ethics*], in the former of which empirical principles constitute the entire foundation, while in the second they do not form the smallest part of it, is the first and most important office of the analytic of pure practical reason; and it must proceed in it with as much *exactness* and, so to speak, *scrupulousness* as any geometer in his work. The philosopher, however, has greater difficulties to contend with here (as always in rational cognition by means of concepts merely without construction), because he cannot take any intuition as a foundation (for a pure noumenon). He has, however, this advantage that, like the chemist, he can at any time make an experiment with every man's practical reason for the purpose of distinguishing the moral (pure) principle of determination from the empirical, namely, by adding the moral law (as a determining principle) to the empirically affected will (*e.g.* that of the man who would be ready to lie because he can gain something thereby). It is as if the analyst added alkali to a solution of lime in hydrochloric acid, the acid at once forsakes the lime, combines with the alkali, and the lime is precipitated. Just in the same way, if to a man who is otherwise honest (or who for this occasion places himself only in thought in the position of an honest man), we present the moral law by which he recognizes the worthlessness of the liar, his practical reason (in forming a judgment of what ought to be done) at once forsakes the advantage, combines with that which maintains in him respect for his own person (truthfulness), and the advantage after it has been separated and washed from every particle of reason (which is altogether on the side of duty) is easily weighed by everyone, so that it can enter into combination with reason in other cases, only not where it could be opposed to the moral law, which reason never forsakes, but most closely unites itself with.

But it does not follow that this distinction between the principle of happiness and that of morality is an *opposition* between them, and pure practical reason does not require that we should *renounce* all claim to happiness, but only that the moment duty is in question we should take *no account* of happiness. It may even in certain respects be a duty to provide for happiness; partly, because (including skill, wealth, riches) it contains means for the fulfilment of our duty; partly, because the absence of it (*e.g.* poverty) implies temptation to transgress our duty. But it can never be an immediate duty to promote our happiness, still less can it be the principle of all duty. Now, as all determining principles of the will, except the law of pure practical reason alone (the moral law) are all empirical, and therefore, as such belong to the principle of happiness, they must all be kept apart from the supreme principle of morality, and never be incorporated with it as a condition; since this would be to destroy all moral worth just as much as any empirical admixture with geometrical principles would destroy the certainty of mathematical evidence, which in Plato's opinion is the most excellent thing in mathematics, even surpassing their utility.

Instead, however, of the Deduction of the supreme principle of pure practical reason, that is, the explanation of the possibility of such a knowledge *à priori*, the utmost we were able to do was to show that if we saw the possibility of the freedom of an efficient cause, we should also see not merely the possibility, but even the necessity of the moral law as the supreme practical law of rational beings, to whom we attribute freedom of causality of their will; because both concepts are so inseparably united, that we might define practical freedom as independence of the will on anything but the moral law. But we cannot perceive the possibility of the freedom of an efficient cause, especially in the world of sense; we are fortunate if only we can be sufficiently assured that there is no proof of its impossibility, and are now by the moral law which postulates it compelled, and therefore authorized to assume it. However, there are still many who think that they can explain this freedom on empirical principles, like any other physical faculty, and treat it as a *psychological* property, the explanation of which only requires a more exact study of the *nature of the soul* and of the motives of the will, and not as a *transcendental* predicate of the causality of a being that belongs to the world of sense (which is really the point). They thus deprive us of the grand revelation which we obtain through practical reason by means of the moral law, the revelation, namely, of a supersensible world by the realization of the otherwise transcendent concept of freedom, and by this deprive us also of the moral law itself, which admits no empirical principle of determination. Therefore it will be necessary to add something here as a protection against this delusion, and to exhibit *empiricism* in its naked superficiality.

The notion of causality as *physical necessity*, in opposition to the same notion as *freedom*, concerns only the existence of things so far as it is *determinable in time*, and, consequently, as phenomena, in opposition to their causality as things in themselves. Now if we take the attributes of existence of things in time for attributes of things in themselves (which is the common view), then it is impossible to reconcile the necessity of the causal relation with freedom; they are contradictory. For from the former it follows that every event, and consequently every action that takes place at a certain point of time, is a necessary result of what existed in time preceding. Now as time past is no longer in my power, hence every action that I perform must be the necessary result of certain determining grounds *which are not in my power*, that is, at the moment in which I am acting I am never free. Nay, even if I assume that my whole existence is independent on any foreign cause (for instance, God), so that the determining principles of my causality, and even of my whole existence, were not outside myself, yet this would not in the least transform that physical necessity into freedom. For at every moment of time I am still under the necessity of being determined to action by that which is *not in my power*, and the series of events infinite *a parte priori* which I only continue according to a pre-determined order, and could never begin of myself, would be a continuous physical chain, and therefore my causality would never be freedom.

If, then, we would attribute freedom to a being whose existence is determined in time, we cannot except him from the law of necessity as to all events in his existence, and consequently as to his actions also; for that would be to hand him over to blind chance. Now as this law inevitably applies to all the causality of things, so far as their *existence* is determinable *in time*, it follows that if this were the mode in which we had also to conceive the *existence of these things in themselves*, freedom must be rejected as a vain and impossible conception. Consequently, if we would still save it, no other way remains but to consider that the existence of a thing, so far as it is determinable in time, and therefore its causality, according to the law of physical necessity, belong to *appearance*, and to attribute *freedom to the same being as a thing in itself.* This is certainly inevitable, if we would retain both these contradictory concepts together; but in application when we try to explain their combination in one and the same action, great difficulties present themselves which seem to render such a combination impracticable.

When I say of a man who commits a theft that, by the physical law of causality, this deed is a necessary result of the determining causes in preceding time, then it was impossible that it could not have happened; how then can the judgment, according to the moral law, make any change, and suppose that it could have been omitted, because the law says that it ought to have been omitted: that is, how can a man be called quite free at the same moment, and with respect to the same action in which he is subject to an inevitable physical necessity? Some try to evade this by saying that the causes that determine his causality are of such a *kind* as to agree with a *comparative* notion of freedom. According to this, that is sometimes called a free effect, the determining physical cause of which lies *within* in the acting thing itself, *e.g.* that which a projectile performs when it is in free motion, in which case we use the word "freedom," because while it is in flight it is not urged by anything external; or as we call the motion of a clock a free motion, because it moves its hands itself, which therefore do not require to be pushed by external force; so although the actions of man are necessarily determined by causes which precede in time, we yet call them free, because these causes are ideas produced by our own faculties, whereby desires are evoked on occasion of circumstances, and hence actions are wrought according to our own pleasure. This is a wretched subterfuge with which some persons still let themselves be put off, and so think they have solved, with a petty word-jugglery, that difficult problem, at the solution of which centuries have laboured in vain, and which can therefore scarcely be found so completely on the surface. In fact, in the question about the freedom which must be the foundation of all moral laws and the consequent responsibility, it does not matter whether the principles which necessarily determine causality by a physical law reside *within* the subject or *without* him, or in the former case whether these principles are instinctive or are conceived by reason, if, as is admitted by these men themselves, these determining ideas have the ground of their existence in time and in the *antecedent state*, and this again in an antecedent, &c. Then it matters not that these are internal; it matters not that they have a psychological and not a mechanical causality, that is, produce actions by means of ideas, and not by bodily movements; they are still *determining principles* of the causality of a being whose existence is determinable in time, and therefore under the necessitation of conditions of past time, which therefore, when the subject has to act, are *no longer in his power*. This may imply psychological freedom (if we choose to apply this term to a merely internal chain of ideas in the mind), but it involves physical necessity, and therefore leaves no room for *transcendental freedom*, which must be conceived as independence on everything empirical, and, consequently, on nature generally, whether it is an object of the internal sense considered in time only, or of the external in time and space. Without this freedom (in the latter and true sense), which alone is practical *à priori*, no moral law and no moral imputation are possible. Just for this reason the necessity of events in time, according to the physical law of causality, may be called the *mechanism* of nature, although we do not mean by this that things which are subject to it must be really material *machines*. We look here only to the necessity of the connexion of events in a time-series as it is developed according to the physical law, whether the subject in which this development takes place is called *automaton materiale* when the mechanical being is moved by matter, or with Leibnitz *spirituale* when it is impelled by ideas; and if the freedom of our will were no other than the latter (say the psychological and comparative, not also transcendental, that is, absolute), then it would at bottom be nothing better than the freedom of a turnspit, which, when once it is wound up, accomplishes its motions of itself.

Now, in order to remove in the supposed case the apparent contradiction between freedom and the mechanism of nature in one and the same action, we must remember what was said in the Critique of Pure Reason, or what follows therefrom, viz. that the necessity of nature, which cannot co-exist with the freedom of the subject, appertains only to the attributes of the thing that is subject to time-conditions, consequently only to those[8] of the acting subject as a phenomenon; that therefore in this respect the determining principles of every action of the same reside in what belongs to past time, and *is no longer in his power* (in which must be included his own past actions and the character that these may determine for him in his own eyes as a phenomenon). But the very same subject being on the other side conscious of himself as a thing in himself, considers his existence also *in so far as it is not subject to time-conditions*, and regards himself as only determinable by laws which he gives himself through reason; and in this his existence nothing is antecedent to the determination of his will, but every action, and in general every modification of his existence, varying according to his internal sense, even the whole series of his existence as a sensible being, is in the consciousness of his supersensible existence nothing but the result, and never to be regarded as the determining principle, of his causality as a *noumenon*. In this view now the rational being can justly say of every unlawful action that he performs, that he could very well have left it undone; although as appearance it is sufficiently determined in the past, and in this respect is absolutely necessary, for it, with all the past which determines it, belongs to the one single phenomenon of his character which he makes for himself, in consequence of which he imputes the causality of those appearances to himself as a cause independent on sensibility.

With this agree perfectly the judicial sentences of that wonderful faculty in us which we call conscience.[9] A man may use as much art as he likes in order to paint to himself an unlawful act that he remembers, as an unintentional error, a mere oversight, such as one can never altogether avoid, and therefore as something in which he was carried away by the stream of physical necessity, and thus to make himself out innocent, yet he finds that the advocate who speaks in his favour can by no means silence the accuser within, if only he is conscious that at the time when he did this wrong he was in his senses, that is, in possession of his freedom; and, nevertheless, he accounts for his error from some bad habits, which by gradual neglect of attention he has allowed to grow upon him to such a degree that he can regard his error as its natural consequence, although this cannot protect him from the blame and reproach which he casts upon himself. This is also the ground of repentance for a long past action at every recollection of it; a painful feeling produced by the moral sentiment, and which is practically void in so far as it cannot serve to undo what has been done. (Hence *Priestley*, as a true and consistent *fatalist*, declares it absurd, and he deserves to be commended for this candour more than those who, while they maintain the mechanism of the will in fact, and its freedom in words only, yet wish it to be thought that they include it in their system of compromise, although they do not explain the possibility of such moral imputation.) But the pain is quite legitimate, because when the law of our intelligible [supersensible] existence (the moral law) is in question, reason recognizes no distinction of time, and only asks whether the event belongs to me, as my act, and then always morally connects the same feeling with it, whether it has happened just now or long ago. For in reference to the *supersensible* consciousness of its existence (*i.e.* freedom) the *life of sense* is but a single phenomenon, which, inasmuch as it contains merely manifestations of the mental disposition with regard to the moral law (*i.e.* of the character), must be judged not according to the physical necessity that belongs to it as phenomenon, but according to the absolute spontaneity of freedom. It may therefore be admitted that if it were possible to have so profound an insight into a man's mental character as shown by internal as well as external actions, as to know all its motives, even the smallest, and likewise all the external occasions that can influence them, we could calculate a man's conduct for the future with as great certainty as a lunar or solar eclipse; and nevertheless we may maintain that the man is free. In fact, if we were capable of a further glance, namely, an intellectual intuition of the same subject (which indeed is not granted to us, and instead of it we have only the rational concept), then we should perceive that this whole chain of appearances in regard to all that concerns the moral laws depends on the spontaneity of the subject as a thing in itself, of the determination of which no physical explanation can be given. In default of this intuition the moral law assures us of this distinction between the relation of our actions as appearance to our sensible nature, and the relation of this sensible nature to the supersensible substratum in us. In this view, which is natural to our reason, though inexplicable, we can also justify some judgments which we passed with all conscientiousness, and which yet at first sight seem quite opposed to all equity. There are cases in which men, even with the same education which has been profitable to others, yet show such early depravity, and so continue to progress in it to years of manhood, that they are thought to be born villains, and their character altogether incapable of improvement; and nevertheless they are judged for what they do or leave undone, they are reproached for their faults as guilty; nay, they themselves (the children) regard these reproaches as well founded, exactly as if in spite of the hopeless natural quality of mind ascribed to them, they remained just as responsible as any other man. This could not happen if we did not suppose that whatever springs from a man's choice (as every action intentionally performed undoubtedly does) has as its foundation a free causality, which from early youth expresses its character in its manifestations (*i.e.* actions). These, on account of the uniformity of conduct, exhibit a natural connexion, which, however, does not make the vicious quality of the will necessary, but, on the contrary, is the consequence of the evil principles voluntarily adopted and unchangeable, which only make it so much the more culpable and deserving of punishment. There still remains a difficulty in the combination of freedom with the mechanism of nature in a being belonging to the world of sense: a difficulty which, even after all the foregoing is admitted, threatens freedom with complete destruction. But with this danger there is also a circumstance that offers hope of an issue still favourable to freedom, namely, that the same difficulty presses much more strongly (in fact, as we shall presently see, presses only) on the system that holds the existence determinable in time and space to be the existence of things in themselves; it does not therefore oblige us to give up[10] our capital supposition of the ideality of time as a mere form of sensible intuition, and consequently as a mere manner of representation which is proper to the subject as belonging to the world of sense; and therefore it only requires that this view be reconciled with this idea [of freedom].

The difficulty is as follows:—Even if it is admitted that the supersensible subject can be free with respect to a given action, although as a subject also belonging to the world of sense, he is under mechanical conditions with respect to the same action; still, as soon as we allow that *God* as universal first cause is also *the cause of the existence of substance* (a proposition which can never be given up without at the same time giving up the notion of God as the Being of all beings, and therewith giving up His all-sufficiency, on which everything in theology depends), it seems as if we must admit that a man's actions have their determining principle in something *which is wholly out of his power*, namely, in the causality of a Supreme Being distinct from himself, and on whom his own existence and the whole determination of his causality are absolutely dependent. In point of fact, if a man's actions as belonging to his modifications in time were not merely modifications of him as appearance, but as a thing in itself, freedom could not be saved. Man would be a marionette or an automaton, like Vaucanson's,[11] prepared and wound up by the Supreme Artist. Self-consciousness would indeed make him a thinking automaton; but the consciousness of his own spontaneity would be mere delusion if this were mistaken for freedom, and it would deserve this name only in a comparative sense, since, although the proximate determining causes of its motion and a long series of their determining causes are internal, yet the last and highest is found in a foreign land. Therefore I do not see how those who still insist on regarding time and space as attributes belonging to the existence of things inthemselves, can avoid admitting the fatality of actions; or if (like the otherwise acute Mendelssohn[12]) they allow them to be conditions necessarily belonging to the existence of finite and derived beings, but not to that of the infinite Supreme Being, I do not see on what ground they can justify such a distinction, or, indeed, how they can avoid the contradiction that meets them, when they hold that existence in time is an attribute necessarily belonging to finite things in themselves, whereas God is the cause of this existence, but cannot be the cause of time (or space) itself (since this must [on this hypothesis] be presupposed as a necessary *à priori* condition of the existence of things); and consequently as regards the existence of these things His causality must be subject to conditions, and even to the condition of time; and this would inevitably bring in everything contradictory to the notions of His infinity and independence. On the other hand, it is quite easy for us to draw the distinction between the attribute of the divine existence of being independent on all time-conditions, and that of a being of the world of sense, the distinction being that between the *existence of a being in itself* and that of a *thing in appearance*. Hence, if this ideality of time and space is not adopted, nothing remains but *Spinozism*, in which space and time are essential attributes of the Supreme Being Himself, and the things dependent on Him (ourselves, therefore, included) are not substances, but merely accidents inhering in Him; since, if these things as His effects exist *in time* only, this being the condition of their existence in themselves, then the actions of these beings must be simply His actions which He performs in some place and time. Thus, Spinozism, in spite of the absurdity of its fundamental idea, argues more consistently than the creation theory can, when beings assumed to be substances, and beings in themselves *existing in time*, are regarded as effects of a Supreme Cause, and yet as not [belonging] to Him and His action, but as separate substances.

The above-mentioned difficulty is resolved briefly and clearly as follows:—If existence *in time* is a mere sensible mode of representation belonging to thinking beings in the world, and consequently does not apply to them as things in themselves, then the creation of these beings is a creation of things in themselves, since the notion of creation does not belong to the sensible form of representation of existence or to causality, but can only be referred to noumena. Consequently, when I say of beings in the world of sense that they are created, I so far regard them as noumena. As it would be a contradiction, therefore, to say that God is a creator of appearances, so also it is a contradiction to say that as creator He is the cause of actions in the world of sense, and therefore as appearances, although He is the cause of the existence of the acting beings (which are noumena). If now it is possible to affirm freedom in spite of the natural mechanism of actions as appearances (by regarding existence in time as something that belongs only to appearances, not to things in themselves), then the circumstance that the acting beings are creatures cannot make the slightest difference, since creation concerns their supersensible and not their sensible existence, and therefore cannot be regarded as the determining principle of the appearances. It would be quite different if the beings in the world as things in themselves existed *in time*, since in that case the creator of substance would be at the same time the author of the whole mechanism of this substance.

Of so great importance is the separation of time (as well as space) from the existence of things in themselves which was effected in the Critique of the Pure Speculative Reason.

It may be said that the solution here proposed involves great difficulty in itself, and is scarcely susceptible of a lucid exposition. But is any other solution that has been attempted, or that may be attempted, easier and more intelligible? Rather might we say that the dogmatic teachers of metaphysics have shown more shrewdness than candour in keeping this difficult point out of sight as much as possible, in the hope that if they said nothing about it, probably no one would think of it. If science is to be advanced, all difficulties must be *laid open*, and we must even search for those that are hidden, for every difficulty calls forth a remedy, which cannot be discovered without science gaining either in extent or in exactness; and thus even obstacles become means of increasing the thoroughness of science. On the other hand, if the difficulties are intentionally concealed, or merely removed by palliatives, then sooner or later they burst out into incurable mischiefs, which bring science to ruin in an absolute scepticism.

Since it is, properly speaking, the notion of freedom alone amongst all the ideas of pure speculative reason that so greatly enlarges our knowledge in the sphere of the supersensible, though only of our practical knowledge, I ask myself *why it exclusively possesses so great fertility*, whereas the others only designate the vacant space for possible beings of the pure understanding, but are unable by any means to define the concept of them. I presently find that as I cannot think anything without a category, I must first look for a category for the Rational Idea of freedom with which I am now concerned; and this is the category of *causality*; and although freedom, a *concept of the reason*, being a transcendent concept, cannot have any intuition corresponding to it, yet the *concept of the understanding*—for the synthesis of which *the former*[13] demands the unconditioned—(namely, the concept of causality) must have a sensible intuition given, by which first its objective reality is assured. Now, the categories are all divided into two classes—the *mathematical*, which concern the unity of synthesis in the conception of objects, and the *dynamical*, which refer to the unity of synthesis in the conception of the existence of objects. The former (those of magnitude and quality) always contain a synthesis of the *homogeneous*; and it is not possible to find in this the unconditioned antecedent to what is given in sensible intuition as conditioned in space and time, as this would itself have to belong to space and time, and therefore be again still conditioned.[14] Whence it resulted in the Dialectic of Pure Theoretic Reason that the opposite methods of attaining the unconditioned and the totality of the conditions were both wrong. The categories of the second class (those of causality and of the necessity of a thing) did not require this homogeneity (of the conditioned and the condition in synthesis), since here what we have to explain is not how the intuition is compounded from a manifold in it, but only how the existence of the conditioned object corresponding to it is added to the existence of the condition (added, namely, in the understanding as connected therewith); and in that case it was allowable to suppose in the supersensible world the unconditioned antecedent to the altogether conditioned in the world of sense (both as regards the causal connexion and the contingent existence of things themselves), although this unconditioned remained indeterminate, and to make the synthesis transcendent. Hence, it was found in the Dialectic of the Pure Speculative Reason that the two apparently opposite methods of obtaining for the conditioned the unconditioned were not really contradictory, *e.g.* in the synthesis of causality to conceive for the conditioned in the series of causes and effects of the sensible world, a causality which has no sensible condition, and that the same action which, as belonging to the world of sense, is always sensibly conditioned, that is, mechanically necessary, yet at the same time may be derived from a causality not sensibly conditioned—being the causality of the acting being as belonging to the supersensible world—and may consequently be conceived as free. Now, the only point in question was to change this *may be* into *is*; that is, that we should be able to show in an actual case, as it were by a fact, that certain actions imply such a causality (namely, the intellectual, sensibly unconditioned), whether they are actual or only commanded, that is, objectively necessary in a practical sense. We could not hope to find this connexion in actions actually given in experience as events of the sensible world, since causality with freedom must always be sought outside the world of sense in the world of intelligence. But things of sense are the only things offered to our perception and observation. Hence, nothing remained but to find an incontestable objective principle of causality which excludes all sensible conditions: that is, a principle in which reason does not appeal further to something *else* as a determining ground of its causality, but contains this determining ground itself by means of that principle, and in which therefore it is itself as *pure reason* practical. Now, this principle had not to be searched for or discovered; it had long been in the reason of all men, and incorporated in their nature, and is the principle of *morality*. Therefore, that unconditioned causality, with the faculty of it, namely, freedom, is no longer merely indefinitely and problematically *thought* (this speculative reason could prove to be feasible), but is even *as regards the law of its causality* definitely and assertorially *known*; and with it the fact that a being (I myself) belonging to the world of sense, belongs also to the supersensible world, this is also positively *known*, and thus the reality of the supersensible world is established, and in practical respects *definitely* given, and this definiteness, which for theoretical purposes would be *transcendent*, is for practical purposes *immanent*. We could not, however, make a similar step as regards the second dynamical idea, namely, that of a *necessary being*. We could not rise to it from the sensible world without the aid of the first dynamical idea. For if we attempted to do so, we should have ventured to leave at a bound all that is given to us, and to leap to that of which nothing is given us that can help us to effect the connexion of such a supersensible being with the world of sense (since the necessary being would have to be known as given *outside ourselves*). On the other hand, it is now obvious that this connexion is quite possible in relation to *our own* subject, inasmuch as I know myself to be *on the one side* as an intelligible [supersensible] being determined by the moral law (by means of freedom), and *on the other side* as acting in the world of sense. It is the concept of freedom alone that enables us to find the unconditioned and intelligible [supersensible] for the conditioned and sensible without going out of ourselves. For it is our own reason that by means of the supreme and unconditional practical law knows that itself and the being that is conscious of this law (our own person) belongs to the pure world of understanding, and moreover defines the manner in which, as such, it can be active. In this way it can be understood why in the whole faculty of reason it is *the practical reason only* that can help us to pass beyond the world of sense, and give us knowledge of a supersensible order and connexion, which, however, for this very reason cannot be extended further than is necessary for pure practical purposes.

Let me be permitted on this occasion to make one more remark, namely, that every step that we make with pure reason, even in the practical sphere where no attention is paid to subtle speculation, nevertheless accords with all the material points of the Critique of the Theoretical Reason as closely and directly as if each step had been thought out with deliberate purpose to establish this confirmation. Such a thorough agreement, wholly unsought for, and quite obvious (as anyone can convince himself, if he will only carry moral inquiries up to their principles), between the most important proposition of practical reason, and the often seemingly too subtle and needless remarks of the Critique of the Speculative Reason, occasions surprise and astonishment, and confirms the maxim already recognized and praised by others, namely, that in every scientific inquiry we should pursue our way steadily with all possible exactness and frankness, without caring for any objections that may be raised from outside its sphere, but, as far as we can, to carry out our inquiry truthfully and completely by itself. Frequent observation has convinced me that when such researches are concluded, that which in one part of them appeared to me very questionable, considered in relation to other extraneous doctrines, when I left this doubtfulness out of sight for a time, and only attended to the business in hand until it was completed, at last was unexpectedly found to agree perfectly with what had been discovered separately without the least regard to those doctrines, and without any partiality or prejudice for them. Authors would save themselves many errors and much labour lost (because spent on a delusion) if they could only resolve to go to work with more frankness.

BOOK II

DIALECTIC OF PURE PRACTICAL REASON

CHAPTER I

OF A DIALECTIC OF PURE PRACTICAL REASON GENERALLY

PURE reason always has its dialectic, whether it is considered in its speculative or its practical employment; for it requires the absolute totality of the conditions of what is given conditioned, and this can only be found in things in themselves. But as all conceptions of things in themselves must be referred to intuitions, and with us men these can never be other than sensible, and hence can never enable us to know objects as things in themselves but only as appearances, and since the unconditioned can never be found in this chain of appearances which consists only of conditioned and conditions; thus from applying this rational idea of the totality of the conditions (in other words, of the unconditioned) to appearances there arises an inevitable illusion, as if these latter were things in themselves (for in the absence of a warning critique they are always regarded as such). This illusion would never be noticed as delusive if it did not betray itself by a *conflict* of reason with itself, when it applies to appearances its fundamental principle of presupposing the unconditioned to everything conditioned. By this, however, reason is compelled to trace this illusion to its source, and search how it can be removed, and this can only be done by a complete critical examination of the whole pure faculty of reason; so that the antinomy of the pure reason which is manifest in its dialectic is in fact the most beneficial error into which human reason could ever have fallen, since it at last drives us to search for the key to escape from this labyrinth; and when this key is found, it further discovers that which we did not seek but yet had need of, namely, a view into a higher and an immutable order of things, in which we even now are, and in which we are thereby enabled by definite precepts to continue to live according to the highest dictates of reason.

It may be seen in detail in the Critique of Pure Reason how in its speculative employment this natural dialectic is to be solved, and how the error which arises from a very natural illusion may be guarded against. But reason in its practical use is not a whit better off. As pure practical reason, it likewise seeks to find the unconditioned for the practically conditioned (which rests on inclinations and natural wants), and this not as the determining principle of the will, but even when this is given (in the moral law) it seeks the unconditioned totality of the *object* of pure practical reason under the name of the *Summum Bonum*.

To define this idea practically, *i.e.* sufficiently for the maxims of our rational conduct, is the business of *practical wisdom* [*Weisheitslehre*], and this again as a science is *philosophy*, in the sense in which the word was understood by the ancients, with whom it meant instruction in the conception in which the *summum bonum* was to be placed, and the conduct by which it was to be obtained. It would be well to leave this word in its ancient signification as a *doctrine of the summum bonum*, so far as reason endeavours to make this into a *science*. For on the one hand the restriction annexed would suit the Greek expression (which signifies the love of *wisdom*), and yet at the same time would be sufficient to embrace under the name of philosophy the love of *science:* that is to say, of all speculative rational knowledge, so far as it is serviceable to reason, both for that conception and also for the practical principle determining our conduct, without letting out of sight the main end, on account of which alone it can be called a doctrine of practical wisdom. On the other hand, it would be no harm to deter the self-conceit of one who ventures to claim the title of philosopher by holding before him in the very definition a standard of self-estimation which would very much lower his pretensions. For *a teacher of wisdom* would mean something more than a scholar who has not come so far as to guide himself, much less to guide others, with certain expectation of attaining so high an end: it would mean a *master in the knowledge of wisdom,* which implies more than a modest man would claim for himself. Thus philosophy as well as wisdom would always remain an ideal, which objectively is presented complete in reason alone, while subjectively for the person it is only the goal of his unceasing endeavours, and no one would be justified in professing to be in possession of it so as to assume the name of philosopher, who could not also show its infallible effects in his own person as an example (in his self-mastery and the unquestioned interest that he takes pre-eminently in the general good), and this the ancients also required as a condition of deserving that honourable title.

We have another preliminary remark to make respecting the dialectic of the pure practical reason, on the point of the definition *of the summum bonum* (a successful solution of which dialectic would lead us to expect, as in case of that of the theoretical reason, the most beneficial effects, inasmuch as the self-contradictions of pure practical reason honestly stated, and not concealed, force us to undertake a complete critique of this faculty).

The moral law is the sole determining principle of a pure will. But since this is merely formal (viz. as prescribing only the form of the maxim as universally legislative), it abstracts as a determining principle from all matter—that is to say, from every object of volition. Hence, though the *summum bonum* may be the whole *object* of a pure practical reason, *i.e.* a pure will, yet it is not on that account to be regarded as its *determining principle,* and the moral law alone must be regarded as the principle on which that and its realization or promotion are aimed at. This remark is important in so delicate a case as the determination of moral principles, where the slightest misinterpretation perverts men's minds. For it will have been seen from the Analytic, that if we assume any object under the name of a good as a determining principle of the will prior to the moral law, and then deduce from it the supreme practical principle, this would always introduce heteronomy, and crush out the moral principle.

It is, however, evident that if the notion of the *summum bonum* includes that of the moral law as its supreme condition, then the *summum bonum* would not merely be an *object*, but the notion of it and the conception of its existence as possible by our own practical reason would likewise be the *determining principle* of the will, since in that case the will is in fact determined by the moral law which is already included in this conception, and by no other object, as the principle of autonomy requires. This order of the conceptions of determination of the will must not be lost sight of, as otherwise we should misunderstand ourselves, and think we had fallen into a contradiction, while everything remains in perfect harmony.

CHAPTER II

OF THE DIALECTIC OF PURE REASON IN DEFINING THE CONCEPTION OF THE "SUMMUM BONUM."

THE conception of the *summum* itself contains an ambiguity which might occasion needless disputes if we did not attend to it. The *summum* may mean either the supreme (*supremum*) or the perfect (*consummatum*). The former is that condition which is itself unconditioned, *i.e.* is not subordinate to any other (*originarium*); the second is that whole which is not a part of a greater whole of the same kind (*perfectissimum*). It has been shown in the Analytic that *virtue* (as worthiness to be happy) is the *supreme condition* of all that can appear to us desirable, and consequently of all our pursuit of happiness, and is therefore the *supreme* good. But it does not follow that it is the whole and perfect good as the object of the desires of rational finite beings; for this requires happiness also, and that not merely in the partial eyes of the person who makes himself an end, but even in the judgment of an impartial reason, which regards persons in general as ends in themselves. For to need happiness, to deserve it, and yet at the same time not to participate in it, cannot be consistent with the perfect volition of a rational being possessed at the same time of all power, if, for the sake of experiment, we conceive such a being. Now inasmuch as virtue and happiness together constitute the possession of the *summum bonum* in a person, and the distribution of happiness in exact proportion to morality (which is the worth of the person, and his worthiness to be happy) constitutes the *summum bonum* of a possible world; hence this *summum bonum* expresses the whole, the perfect good, in which, however, virtue as the condition is always the supreme good, since it has no condition above it; whereas happiness, while it is pleasant to the possessor of it, is not of itself absolutely and in all respects good, but always presupposes morally right behaviour as its condition.

When two elements are *necessarily* united in one concept, they must be connected as reason and consequence, and this either so that their unity is considered as *analytical* (logical connexion), or as *synthetical* (real connexion)—the former following the law of identity, the latter that of causality. The connexion of virtue and happiness may therefore be understood in two ways: either the endeavour to be virtuous and the rational pursuit of happiness are not two distinct actions, but absolutely identical, in which case no maxim need be made the principle of the former, other than what serves for the latter; or the connexion consists in this, that virtue produces happiness as something distinct from the consciousness of virtue, as a cause produces an effect.

The ancient Greek schools were, properly speaking, only two, and in determining the conception of the *summum bonum* these followed in fact one and the same method, inasmuch as they did not allow virtue and happiness to be regarded as two distinct elements of the *summum bonum,* and consequently sought the unity of the principle by the rule of identity; but they differed as to which of the two was to be taken as the fundamental notion. The *Epicurean* said: To be conscious that one's maxims lead to happiness is virtue; the *Stoic* said: To be conscious of one's virtue is happiness. With the former, *Prudence* was equivalent to morality; with the latter, who chose a higher designation for virtue, morality alone was true wisdom.

While we must admire the men who in such early times tried all imaginable ways of extending the domain of philosophy, we must at the same time lament that their acuteness was unfortunately misapplied in trying to trace out identity between two extremely heterogeneous notions, those of happiness and virtue. But it agrees with the dialectical spirit of their times (and subtle minds are even now sometimes misled in the same way) to get rid of irreconcilable differences in principle by seeking to change them into a mere contest about words, and thus apparently working out the identity of the notion under different names, and this usually occurs in cases where the combination of heterogeneous principles lies so deep or so high, or would require so complete a transformation of the doctrines assumed in the rest of the philosophical system, that men are afraid to penetrate deeply into the real difference, and prefer treating it as a difference in matters of form.

While both schools sought to trace out the identity of the practical principles of virtue and happiness, they were not agreed as to the way in which they tried to force this identity, but were separated infinitely from one another, the one placing its principle on the side of sense, the other on that of reason; the one in the consciousness of sensible wants, the other in the independence of practical reason on all sensible grounds of determination. According to the Epicurean the notion of virtue was already involved in the maxim: To promote one's own happiness; according to the Stoics, on the other hand, the feeling of happiness was already contained in the consciousness of virtue. Now whatever is contained in another notion is identical with part of the containing notion, but not with the whole, and moreover two wholes may be specifically distinct, although they consist of the same parts, namely, if the parts are united into a whole in totally different ways. The Stoic maintained that virtue was the *whole summum bonum,* and happiness only the consciousness of possessing it, as making part of the state of the subject. The Epicurean maintained that happiness was the *whole summum bonum,* and virtue only the form of the maxim for its pursuit, viz. the rational use of the means for attaining it.

Now it is clear from the Analytic that the maxims of virtue and those of private happiness are quite heterogeneous as to their supreme practical principle; and although they belong to one *summum bonum* which together they make possible, yet they are so far from coinciding that they restrict and check one another very much in the same subject. Thus the question, *How is the summum bonum* practically possible? still remains an unsolved problem, notwithstanding all the *attempts at coalition* that have hitherto been made. The Analytic has, however, shown what it is that makes the problem difficult to solve; namely, that happiness and morality are two specifically *distinct elements of the summum bonum*, and therefore their combination *cannot* be *analytically* cognized (as if the man that seeks his own happiness should find by mere analysis of his conception that in so acting he is virtuous, or as if the man that follows virtue should in the consciousness of such conduct find that he is already happy *ipso facto*) but must be a *synthesis* of concepts. Now since this combination is recognized as *à priori*, and therefore as practically necessary, and consequently not as derived from experience, so that the possibility of the *summum bonum* does not rest on any empirical principle, it follows that the *deduction* [legitimation] of this concept must be *transcendental*. It is *à priori* (morally) necessary to *produce the summum bonum by freedom of will:* therefore the condition of its possibility must rest solely on *à priori* principles of cognition.

I.—*The Antinomy of Practical Reason*

In the *summum bonum* which is practical for us, *i.e.* to be realized by our will, virtue and happiness are thought as necessarily combined, so that the one cannot be assumed by pure practical reason without the other also being attached to it. Now this combination (like every other) is either *analytical* or *synthetical*. It has been shown that it cannot be analytical; it must then be synthetical, and, more particularly, must be conceived as the connexion of cause and effect, since it concerns a practical good, *i.e.* one that is possible by means of action; consequently either the desire of happiness must be the motive to maxims of virtue, or the maxim of virtue must be the efficient cause of happiness. The first is *absolutely* impossible, because (as was proved in the Analytic) maxims which place the determining principle of the will in the desire of personal happiness are not moral at all, and no virtue can be founded on them. But the second is *also impossible*, because the practical connexion of causes and effects in the world, as the result of the determination of the will, does not depend upon the moral dispositions of the will, but on the knowledge of the laws of nature and the physical power to use them for one's purposes; consequently we cannot expect in the world by the most punctilious observance of the moral laws any necessary connexion of happiness with virtue adequate to the *summum bonum*. Now as the promotion of this *summum bonum*, the conception of which contains this connexion, is *à priori* a necessary object of our will, and inseparably attached to the moral law, the impossibility of the former must prove the falsity of the latter. If then the supreme good is not possible by practical rules, then the moral law also which commands us to promote it is directed to vain imaginary ends, and must consequently be false.

II.—*Critical Solution of the Antinomy of Practical Reason*

The antinomy of pure speculative reason exhibits a similar conflict between freedom and physical necessity in the causality of events in the world. It was solved by showing that there is no real contradiction when the events and even the world in which they occur are regarded (as they ought to be) merely as appearances; since one and the same acting being, *as an appearance* (even to his own inner sense), has a causality in the world of sense that always conforms to the mechanism of nature, but with respect to the same events, so far as the acting person regards himself at the same time as a noumenon (as pure intelligence in an existence not dependent on the condition of time), he can contain a principle by which that causality acting according to laws of nature is determined, but which is itself free from all laws of nature.

It is just the same with the foregoing antinomy of pure practical reason. The first of the two propositions—That the endeavour after happiness produces a virtuous mind, is *absolutely false*; but the second, That a virtuous mind necessarily produces happiness, is *not absolutely* false, but only in so far as virtue is considered as a form of causality in the sensible world, and consequently only if I suppose existence in it to be the only sort of existence of a rational being; it is then only *conditionally* false. But as I am not only justified in thinking that I exist also as a noumenon in a world of the understanding, but even have in the moral law a purely intellectual determining principle of my causality (in the sensible world), it is not impossible that morality of mind should have a connexion as cause with happiness (as an effect in the sensible world) if not immediate yet mediate (viz.: through an intelligent author of nature), and moreover necessary; while in a system of nature which is merely an object of the senses this combination could never occur except contingently, and therefore could not suffice for the *summum bonum*.

Thus, notwithstanding this seeming conflict of practical reason with itself, the *summum bonum*, which is the necessary supreme end of a will morally determined, is a true object thereof; for it is practically possible, and the maxims of the will which as regards their matter refer to it have objective reality, which at first was threatened by the antinomy that appeared in the connexion of morality with happiness by a general law; but this was merely from a misconception, because the relation between appearances was taken for a relation of the things in themselves to these appearances.

When we find ourselves obliged to go so far, namely, to the connexion with an intelligible world, to find the possibility of the *summum bonum*, which reason points out to all rational beings as the goal of all their moral wishes, it must seem strange that, nevertheless, the philosophers both of ancient and modern times have been able to find happiness in accurate proportion to virtue even in *this life* (in the sensible world), or have persuaded themselves that they were conscious thereof. For Epicurus as well as the Stoics extolled above everything the happiness that springs from the consciousness of living virtuously; and the former was not so base in his practical precepts as one might infer from the principles of his theory, which he used for explanation and not for action, or as they were interpreted by many who were misled by his using the term pleasure for contentment; on the contrary, he reckoned the most disinterested practice of good amongst the ways of enjoying the most intimate delight, and his scheme of pleasure (by which he meant constant cheerfulness of mind) included the moderation and control of the inclinations, such as the strictest moral philosopher might require. He differed from the Stoics chiefly in making this pleasure the motive, which they very rightly refused to do. For, on the one hand, the virtuous Epicurus, like many well-intentioned men of this day, who do not reflect deeply enough on their principles, fell into the error of presupposing the virtuous *disposition* in the persons for whom he wished to provide the springs to virtue (and indeed the upright man cannot he happy if he is not first conscious of his uprightness; since with such a character the reproach that his habit of thought would oblige him to make against himself in case of transgression and his moral self-condemnation would rob him of all enjoyment of the pleasantness which his condition might otherwise contain). But the question is, How is such a disposition possible in the first instance, and such a habit of thought in estimating the worth of one's existence, since prior to it there can be in the subject no feeling at all for moral worth? If a man is virtuous without being conscious of his integrity in every action, he will certainly not enjoy life, however favourable fortune may be to him in its physical circumstances; but can we make him virtuous in the first instance, in other words, before he esteems the moral worth of his existence so highly, by praising to him the peace of mind that would result from the consciousness of an integrity for which he has no sense?

On the other hand, however, there is here an occasion of a *vitium subreptionis,* and as it were of an optical illusion, in the self-consciousness of what one *does* as distinguished from what one *feels*—an illusion which even the most experienced cannot altogether avoid. The moral disposition of mind is necessarily combined with a consciousness that the will is determined *directly by the law.* Now the consciousness of a determination of the faculty of desire is always the source of a satisfaction in the resulting action; but this pleasure, this satisfaction in oneself, is not the determining principle of the action; on the contrary, the determination of the will directly by reason is the source of the feeling of pleasure, and this remains a pure practical not sensible determination of the faculty of desire. Now as this determination has exactly the same effect within in impelling to activity, that a feeling of the pleasure to be expected from the desired action would have had, we easily look on what we ourselves do as something which we merely passively feel, and take the moral spring for a sensible impulse, just as it happens in the so-called illusion of the senses (in this case the inner sense). It is a sublime thing in human nature to be determined to actions immediately by a purely rational law; sublime even is the illusion that regards the subjective side of this capacity of intellectual determination as something sensible, and the effect of a special sensible feeling (for an intellectual feeling would be a contradiction). It is also of great importance to attend to this property of our personality, and as much as possible to cultivate the effect of reason on this feeling. But we must beware lest by falsely extolling this moral determining principle as a spring, making its source lie in particular feelings of pleasure (which are in fact only results), we degrade and disfigure the true genuine spring, the law itself, by putting as it were a false foil upon it. Respect, not pleasure or enjoyment of happiness, is something for which it is not possible that reason should have any *antecedent* feeling as its foundation (for this would always be sensible and pathological); [and][1] consciousness of immediate obligation of the will by the law is by no means analogous to the feeling of pleasure, although in relation to the faculty of desire it produces the same effect, but from different sources: it is only by this mode of conception, however, that we can attain what we are seeking, namely, that actions be done not merely in accordance with duty (as a result of pleasant feelings), but from duty, which must be the true end of all moral cultivation.

Have we not, however, a word which does not express enjoyment, as happiness does, but indicates a satisfaction in one's existence, an analogue of the happiness which must necessarily accompany the consciousness of virtue? Yes! this word is *self-contentment*, which in its proper signification always designates only a negative satisfaction in one's existence, in which one is conscious of needing nothing. Freedom and the consciousness of it as a faculty of following the moral law with unyielding resolution is *independence on inclinations*, at least as motives determining (though not as *affecting)* our desire, and so far as I am conscious of this freedom in following my moral maxims, it is the only source of an unaltered contentment which is necessarily connected with it and rests on no special feeling. This may be called intellectual contentment. The sensible contentment (improperly so-called) which rests on the satisfaction of the inclinations, however delicate they may be imagined to be, can never be adequate to the conception of it. For the inclinations change, they grow with the indulgence shown them, and always leave behind a still greater void than we had thought to fill. Hence they are always *burdensome* to a rational being, and although he cannot lay them aside, they wrest from him the wish to be rid of them. Even an inclination to what is right (*e.g.* to beneficence), though it may much facilitate the efficacy of the *moral* maxims, cannot produce any. For in these all must be directed to the conception of the law as a determining principle, if the action is to contain *morality* and not merely *legality*. Inclination is blind and slavish whether it be of a good sort or not and when morality is in question, reason must not play the part merely of guardian to inclination, but, disregarding it altogether, must attend simply to its own interest as pure practical reason. This very feeling of compassion and tender sympathy, if it precedes the deliberation on the question of duty and becomes a determining principle, is even annoying to right-thinking persons, brings their deliberate maxims into confusion, and makes them wish to be delivered from it and to be subject to law-giving reason alone.

From this we can understand how the consciousness of this faculty of a pure practical reason produces by action (virtue) a consciousness of mastery over one's inclinations, and therefore of independence on them, and consequently also on the discontent that always accompanies them, and thus a negative satisfaction with one's state, i.e. *contentment*, which is primarily contentment with one's own person. Freedom itself becomes in this way (namely indirectly) capable of an enjoyment which cannot be called happiness, because it does not depend on the positive concurrence of a feeling, nor is it, strictly speaking, *bliss*, since it does not include complete independence on inclinations and wants, but it resembles bliss in so far as the determination of one's will at least can hold itself free from their influence; and thus, at least in its origin, this enjoyment is analogous to the self-sufficiency which we can ascribe only to the Supreme Being.

From this solution of the antinomy of pure practical reason it follows that in practical principles we may at least conceive as possible a natural and necessary connexion between the consciousness of morality and the expectation of a proportionate happiness as its result, though it does not follow that we can know or perceive this connexion; that, on the other hand, principles of the pursuit of happiness cannot possibly produce morality; that, therefore, morality is the *supreme* good (as the first condition of the *summum bonum*, while happiness constitutes its second element, but only in such a way that it is the morally conditioned, but necessary consequence of the former. Only with this subordination is the *summum bonum* the whole object of pure practical reason, which must necessarily conceive it as possible, since it commands us to contribute to the utmost of our power to its realization. But since the possibility of such connexion of the conditioned with its condition belongs wholly to the supersensual relation of things, and cannot be given according to the laws of the world of sense, although the practical consequences of the idea belong to the world of sense, namely, the actions that aim at realizing the *summum bonum*; we will therefore endeavour to set forth the grounds of that possibility, first, in respect of what is immediately in our power, and then, secondly, in that which is not in our power, but which reason presents to us as the supplement of our impotence, for the realization of the *summum bonum* (which by practical principles is necessary).

III.—*Of the Primacy of Pure Practical Reason in its Union with the Speculative Reason*

By primacy between two or more things connected by reason, I understand the prerogative belonging to one, of being the first determining principle in the connexion with all the rest. In a narrower practical sense it means the prerogative of the interest of one in so far as the interest of the other is subordinated to it, while it is not postponed to any other. To every faculty of the mind we can attribute an interest, that is a principle that contains the condition on which alone the former is called into exercise. Reason, as the faculty of principles, determines the interest of all the powers of the mind, and is determined by its own. The interest of its speculative employment consists in the *cognition* of the object pushed to the highest *à priori* principles: that of its practical employment, in the determination of the *will* in respect of the final and complete end. As to what is necessary for the possibility of any employment of reason at all, namely, that its principles and affirmations should not contradict one another, this constitutes no part of its interest, but is the condition of having reason at all; it is only its development, not mere consistency with itself, that is reckoned as its interest.

If practical reason could not assume or think as given anything further than what speculative reason of itself could offer it from its own insight, the latter would have the primacy. But supposing that it had of itself original *à priori* principles with which certain theoretical positions were inseparably connected, while these were withdrawn from any possible insight of speculative reason (which, however, they must not contradict); then the question is, which interest is the superior (not which must give way, for they are not necessarily conflicting), whether speculative reason, which knows nothing of all that the practical offers for its acceptance, should take up these propositions, and (although they transcend it) try to unite them with its own concepts as a foreign possession handed over to it, or whether it is justified in obstinately following its own separate interest, and according to the canonic of Epicurus rejecting as vain subtlety everything that cannot accredit its objective reality by manifest examples to be shown in experience, even though it should be never so much interwoven with the interest of the practical (pure) use of reason, and in itself not contradictory to the theoretical, merely because it infringes on the interest of the speculative reason to this extent, that it removes the bounds which this latter had set to itself, and gives it up to every nonsense or delusion of imagination?

In fact, so far as practical reason is taken as dependent on pathological conditions, that is, as merely regulating the inclinations under the sensible principle of happiness, we could not require speculative reason to take its principles from such a source. *Mohammed's* paradise, or the absorption into the Deity of the *theosophists* and *mystics*, would press their monstrosities on the reason according to the taste of each, and one might as well have no reason as surrender it in such fashion to all sorts of dreams. But if pure reason of itself can be practical and is actually so, as the consciousness of the moral law proves, then it is still only one and the same reason which, whether in a theoretical or a practical point of view, judges according to à *priori* principles; and then it is clear that although it is in the first point of view incompetent to establish certain propositions positively, which, however, do not contradict it, then as soon as these propositions are *inseparably* attached *to the practical interest* of pure reason, then it must accept them, though it be as something offered to it from a foreign source, something that has not grown on its own ground, but yet is sufficiently authenticated; and it must try to compare and connect them with everything that it has in its power as speculative reason. It must remember, however, that these are not additions to its insight, but yet are extensions of its employment in another, namely, a practical aspect; and this is not in the least opposed to its interest, which consists in the restriction of wild speculation.

Thus, when pure speculative and pure practical reason are combined in one cognition, the latter has the *primacy*, provided, namely, that this combination is not *contingent* and arbitrary, but founded *à priori* on reason itself and therefore *necessary*. For without this subordination there would arise a conflict of reason with itself; since if they were merely co-ordinate, the former would close its boundaries strictly and admit nothing from the latter into its domain, while the latter would extend its bounds over everything, and when its needs required would seek to embrace the former within them. Nor could we reverse the order, and require pure practical reason to be subordinate to the speculative, since all interest is ultimately practical, and even that of speculative reason is conditional, and it is only in the practical employment of reason that it is complete.

IV.—*The Immortality of the Soul as a Postulate of Pure Practical Reason*

The realization of the *summum bonum* in the world is the necessary object of a will determinable by the moral law. But in this will the *perfect accordance* of the mind with the moral law is the supreme condition of the *summum bonum*. This then must be possible, as well as its object, since it is contained in the command to promote the latter. Now, the perfect accordance of the will with the moral law is *holiness*, a perfection of which no rational being of the sensible world is capable at any moment of his existence. Since, nevertheless, it is required as practically necessary, it can only be found in a *progress in infinitum* towards that perfect accordance, and on the principles of pure practical reason it is necessary to assume such a practical progress as the real object of our will.

Now, this endless progress is only possible on the supposition of an *endless* duration of the *existence* and personality of the same rational being (which is called the immortality of the soul). The *summum bonum*, then, practically is only possible on the supposition of the immortality of the soul; consequently this immortality, being inseparably connected with the moral law, is a postulate of pure practical reason (by which I mean a *theoretical* proposition, not demonstrable as such, but which is an inseparable result of an unconditional *à priori practical* law).[2]

This principle of the moral destination of our nature, namely, that it is only in an endless progress that we can attain perfect accordance with the moral law, is of the greatest use, not merely for the present purpose of supplementing the impotence of speculative reason, but also with respect to religion. In default of it, either the moral law is quite degraded from its *holiness*, being made out to be *indulgent*, and conformable to our convenience, or else men strain their notions of their vocation and their expectation to an unattainable goal, hoping to acquire complete holiness of will, and so they lose themselves in fantastical *theosophic* dreams, which wholly contradict self-knowledge. In both cases the unceasing *effort* to obey punctually and thoroughly a strict and inflexible command of reason, which yet is not ideal but real, is only hindered. For a rational but finite being, the only thing possible is an endless progress from the lower to higher degrees of moral perfection. The *Infinite* Being, to whom the condition of time is nothing, sees in this to us endless succession a whole of accordance with the moral law; and the holiness which His command inexorably requires, in order to be true to His justice in the share which He assigns to each in the *summum bonum*, is to be found in a single intellectual intuition of the whole existence of rational beings. All that can be expected of the creature in respect of the hope of this participation would be the consciousness of his tried character, by which, from the progress he has hitherto made from the worse to the morally better, and the immutability of purpose which has thus become known to him, he may hope for a further unbroken continuance of the same, however long his existence may last, even beyond this life,[3] and thus he may hope, not indeed here, nor in any imaginable point of his future existence, but only in the endlessness of his duration (which God alone can survey) to be perfectly adequate to his will (without indulgence or excuse, which do not harmonize with justice).

V.—*The Existence of God as a Postulate of Pure Practical Reason*

In the foregoing analysis the moral law led to a practical problem which is prescribed by pure reason alone, without the aid of any sensible motives, namely, that of the necessary completeness of the first and principal element of the *summum bonum,* viz. Morality; and as this can be perfectly solved only in eternity, to the postulate of *immortality.* The same law must also lead us to affirm the possibility of the second element of the *summum bonum,* viz. Happiness proportioned to that morality, and this on grounds as disinterested as before, and solely from impartial reason; that is, it must lead to the supposition of the existence of a cause adequate to this effect; in other words, it must postulate the *existence of God,* as the necessary condition of the possibility of the *summum bonum* (an object of the will which is necessarily connected with the moral legislation of pure reason). We proceed to exhibit this connexion in a convincing manner.

Happiness is the condition of a rational being in the world with whom *everything goes according to his wish and will*; it rests, therefore, on the harmony of physical nature with his whole end, and likewise with the essential determining principle of his will. Now the moral law as a law of freedom commands by determining principles, which ought to be quite independent on nature and on its harmony with our faculty of desire (as springs). But the acting rational being in the world is not the cause of the world and of nature itself. There is not the least ground, therefore, in the moral law for a necessary connexion between morality and proportionate happiness in a being that belongs to the world as part of it, and therefore dependent on it, and which for that reason cannot by his will be a cause of this nature, nor by his own power, make it thoroughly harmonize, as far as his happiness is concerned, with his practical principles. Nevertheless, in the practical problem of pure reason, *i.e.* the necessary pursuit of the *summum bonum*, such a connexion is postulated as necessary: we ought to endeavour to promote the *summum bonum*, which, therefore, must be possible. Accordingly, the existence of a cause of all nature, distinct from nature itself, and containing the principle of this connexion, namely, of the exact harmony of happiness with morality, is also *postulated*. Now, this supreme cause must contain the principle of the harmony of nature, not merely with a law of the will of rational beings, but with the conception of this *law*, in so far as they make it the *supreme determining principle of the will*, and consequently not merely with the form of morals, but with their morality as their motive, that is, with their moral character. Therefore, the *summum bonum* is possible in the world only on the supposition of a Supreme Being[5] having a causality corresponding to moral character. Now a being that is capable of acting on the conception of laws is an *intelligence* (a rational being), and the causality of such a being according to this conception of laws is his *will*; therefore the supreme cause of nature, which must be presupposed as a condition of the *summum bonum* is a being which is the cause of nature by *intelligence* and *will*, consequently its author, that is God. It follows that the postulate of the possibility of the *highest derived good* (the best world) is likewise the postulate of the reality of a *highest original good*, that is to say, of the existence of God. Now it was seen to be a duty for us to promote the *summum bonum*; consequently it is not merely allowable, but it is a necessity connected with duty as a requisite, that we should presuppose the possibility of this *summum bonum*; and as this is possible only on condition of the existence of God, it inseparably connects the supposition of this with duty; that is, it is morally necessary to assume the existence of God.

It must be remarked here that this moral necessity is *subjective*, that is, it is a want, and not *objective*, that is, itself a duty, for there cannot be a duty to suppose the existence of anything (since this concerns only the theoretical employment of reason). Moreover, it is not meant by this that it is necessary to suppose the existence of God *as a basis of all obligation in general* (for this rests, as has been sufficiently proved, simply on the autonomy of reason itself). What belongs to duty here is only the endeavour to realize and promote the *summum bonum* in the world, the possibility of which can therefore be postulated; and as our reason finds it not conceivable except on the supposition of a supreme intelligence, the admission of this existence is therefore connected with the consciousness of our duty, although the admission itself belongs to the domain of speculative reason. Considered in respect of this alone, as a principle of explanation, it may be called a *hypothesis*, but in reference to the intelligibility of an object given us by the moral law (the *summum bonum*), and consequently of a requirement for practical purposes, it may be called *faith*, that is to say a pure *rational faith*, since pure reason (both in its theoretical and its practical use) is the sole source from which it springs.

From this *deduction* it is now intelligible why the *Greek* schools could never attain the solution of their problem of the practical possibility of the *summum bonum*, because they made the rule of the use which the will of man makes of his freedom the sole and sufficient ground of this possibility, thinking that they had no need for that purpose of the existence of God. No doubt they were so far right that they established the principle of morals of itself independently on this postulate, from the relation of reason only to the will, and consequently made it the *supreme* practical condition of the *summum bonum*; but it was not therefore the *whole* condition of its possibility. The *Epicureans* had indeed assumed as the supreme principle of morality a wholly false one, namely, that of happiness, and had substituted for a law a maxim of arbitrary choice according to every man's inclination; they proceeded, however, *consistently* enough in this, that they degraded their *summum bonum* likewise just in proportion to the meanness of their fundamental principle, and looked for no greater happiness than can be attained by human prudence (including temperance and moderation of the inclinations), and this, as we know, would be scanty enough and would be very different according to circumstances; not to mention the exceptions that their maxims must perpetually admit and which make them incapable of being laws. The *Stoics*, on the contrary, had chosen their supreme practical principle quite rightly, making virtue the condition of the *summum bonum*; but when they represented the degree of virtue required by its pure law as fully attainable in this life, they not only strained the moral powers of the *man* whom they called *the wise* beyond all the limits of his nature, and assumed a thing that contradicts all our knowledge of men, but also and principally they would not allow the second *element* of the *summum bonum,* namely, happiness, to be properly a special object of human desire, but made their *wise man,* like a divinity in his consciousness of the excellence of his person, wholly independent on nature (as regards his own contentment); they exposed him indeed to the evils of life, but made him not subject to them (at the same time representing him also as free from moral evil). They thus, in fact, left out the second element of the *summum bonum,* namely, personal happiness, placing it solely in action and satisfaction with one's own personal worth, thus including it in the consciousness of being morally minded, in which they might have been sufficiently refuted by the voice of their own nature.

The doctrine of Christianity,[6] even if we do not yet consider it as a religious doctrine, gives, touching this point, a conception of the *summum bonum* (the kingdom of God), which alone satisfies the strictest demand of practical reason. The moral law is holy (unyielding) and demands holiness of morals, although all the moral perfection to which man can attain is still only virtue, that is, a rightful disposition arising from *respect* for the law, implying consciousness of a constant propensity to transgression, or at least a want of purity, that is, a mixture of many spurious (not moral) motives of obedience to the law, consequently a self-esteem combined with humility. In respect, then, of the holiness which the Christian law requires, this leaves the creature nothing but a progress *in infinitum*, but for that very reason it justifies him in hoping for an endless duration of his existence. The *worth* of a character *perfectly* accordant with the moral law is infinite, since the only restriction on all possible happiness in the judgment of a wise and all-powerful distributor of it is the absence of conformity of rational beings to their duty. But the moral law of itself does not *promise* any happiness, for according to our conceptions of an order of nature in general, this is not necessarily connected with obedience to the law. Now Christian morality supplies this defect (of the second indispensable element of the *summum bonum*) by representing the world, in which rational beings devote them-selves with all their soul to the moral law, as a *kingdom of God*, in which nature and morality are brought into a harmony foreign to each of itself, by a holy Author who makes the derived *sum-mum bonum* possible. *Holiness* of life is prescribed to them as a rule even in this life, while the welfare proportioned to it, namely, *bliss*, is represented as attainable only in an eternity; because the *former* must always be the pattern of their conduct in every state, and progress towards it is already possible and neces-sary in this life; while the *latter*, under the name of happiness, cannot be attained at all in this world (so far as our own power is concerned), and therefore is made simply an object of hope. Nevertheless, the Christian principle of *morality* itself is not theo-logical (so as to be heteronomy), but is autonomy of pure practi-cal reason, since it does not make the knowledge of God and His will the foundation of these laws, but only of the attainment of the *summum bonum*, on condition of following these laws, and it does not even place the proper *spring* of this obedience in the desired results, but solely in the conception of duty, as that of which the faithful observance alone constitutes the worthiness to obtain those happy consequences.

In this manner the moral laws lead through the conception of the *summum bonum* as the object and final end of pure practical reason to *religion,* that is, to the *recognition of all duties as divine commands, not as sanctions,*[7] *that is to say, arbitrary ordinances of a foreign will and contingent in themselves,* but as essential *laws* of every free will in itself, which, nevertheless, must be regarded as commands of the Supreme Being, because it is only from a morally perfect (holy and good) and at the same time all-powerful will, and consequently only through harmony with this will, that we can hope to attain the *summum bonum* which the moral law makes it our duty to take as the object of our endeavours. Here again, then, all remains disinterested and founded merely on duty; neither fear nor hope being made the fundamental springs, which if taken as principles would destroy the whole moral worth of actions. The moral law commands me to make the highest possible good in a world the ultimate object of all my conduct. But I cannot hope to effect this otherwise than by the harmony of my will with that of a holy and good Author of the world; and although the conception of the *summum bonum* as a whole, in which the greatest happiness is conceived as combined in the most exact proportion with the highest degree of moral perfection (possible in creatures), includes *my own happiness,* yet it is not this that is the determining principle of the will which is enjoined to promote the *summum bonum,* but the moral law, which, on the contrary, limits by strict conditions my unbounded desire of happiness.

Hence also morality is not properly the doctrine how we should *make* ourselves happy, but how we should become *worthy* of happiness. It is only when religion is added that there also comes in the hope of participating some day in happiness in proportion as we have endeavoured to be not unworthy of it.

A man is *worthy* to possess a thing or a state when his possession of it is in harmony with the *summum bonum*. We can now easily see that all worthiness depends on moral conduct, since in the conception of the *summum bonum* this constitutes the condition of the rest (which belongs to one's state), namely, the participation of happiness. Now it follows from this that *morality* should never be treated as a *doctrine of happiness*, that is, an instruction, how to become happy; for it has to do simply with the rational condition (*conditio sine qua non*) of happiness, not with the means of attaining it. But when morality has been completely expounded (which merely imposes duties instead of providing rules for selfish desires), then first, after the moral desire to promote the *summum bonum* (*to* bring the kingdom of God to us) has been awakened, a desire founded on a law, and which could not previously arise in any selfish mind, and when for the behoof of this desire the step to religion has been taken, then this ethical doctrine may be also called a doctrine of happiness because the *hope* of happiness first begins with religion only.

We can also see from this that, when we ask what is *God's ultimate end* in creating the world, we must not name the *happiness* of the rational beings in it, but the *summum bonum*, which adds a further condition to that wish of such beings, namely, the condition of being worthy of happiness, that is, the *morality* of these same rational beings, a condition which alone contains the rule by which only they can hope to share in the former at the hand of a *wise* Author. For as *wisdom* theoretically considered signifies *the knowledge of the summum bonum*, and practically *the accordance of the will with the summum bonum*, we cannot attribute to a supreme independent wisdom an end based merely on *goodness*. For we cannot conceive the action of this goodness (in respect of the happiness of rational beings) as suitable to the highest original good, except under the restrictive conditions of harmony with the holiness of His will. Therefore those who placed the end of creation in the glory of God (provided that this is not conceived anthropomorphically as a desire to be praised) have perhaps hit upon the best expression. For nothing glorifies God more than that which is the most estimable thing in the world, respect for His command, the observance of the holy duty that His law imposes on us, when there is added thereto His glorious plan of crowning such a beautiful order of things with corresponding happiness. If the latter (to speak humanly) makes Him worthy of love, by the *former* He is an object of adoration. Even men can never acquire respect by benevolence alone, though they may gain love, so that the greatest beneficence only procures them honour when it is regulated by worthiness.

That in the order of ends, man (and with him every rational being) is *an end in himself*, that is, that he can never be used merely as a means by any (not even by God) without being at the same time an end also himself, that therefore *humanity* in our person must be *holy* to ourselves, this follows now of itself because he is the *subject*[8] *of the moral law*, in other words, of that which is holy in itself, and on account of which and in agreement with which alone can anything be termed holy. For this moral law is founded on the autonomy of his will, as a free will which by its universal laws must necessarily be able to agree with that to which it is to submit itself.

VI.—*Of the Postulates of Pure Practical Season in General*

They all proceed from the principle of morality, which is not a postulate but a law, by which reason determines the will directly, which will, because it is so determedin as a pure will, requires these necessary conditions of obedience to its precept. These postulates are not theoretical dogmas but, suppositions practically necessary; while then they do [not] extend our speculative knowledge, they give objective reality to the ideas of speculative reason in general (by means of their reference to what is practical), and give it a right to concepts, the possibility even of which it could not otherwise venture to affirm.

These postulates are those *of immortality, freedom* positively considered (as the causality of a being so far as he belongs to the intelligible world), and the *existence of God.* The *first* results from the practically necessary condition of a duration adequate to the complete fulfilment of the moral law; the *second* from the necessary supposition of independence on the sensible world, and of the faculty of determining one's will according to the law of an intelligible world, that is, of freedom; the *third* from the necessary condition of the existence of the *summum bonum* in such an intelligible world, by the supposition of the supreme independent good, that is, the existence of God.

Thus the fact that respect for the moral law necessarily makes the *summum bonum* an object of our endeavours, and the supposition thence resulting of its objective reality, lead through the postulates of practical reason to conceptions which speculative reason might indeed present as problems, but could never solve. Thus it leads—1. To that one in the solution of which the latter could do nothing but commit *paralogisms* (namely, that of immortality), because it could not lay hold of the character of permanence, by which to complete the psychological conception of an ultimate subject necessarily ascribed to the soul in self-consciousness, so as to make it the real conception of a substance, a character which practical reason furnishes by the postulate of a duration required for accordance with the moral law in the *summum bonum*, which is the whole end of practical reason. 2. It leads to that of which speculative reason contained nothing but *antinomy*, the solution of which it could only found on a notion problematically conceivable indeed, but whose objective reality it could not prove or determine, namely, the *cosmological* idea of an intelligible world and the consciousness of our existence in it, by means of the postulate of freedom (the reality of which it lays down by virtue of the moral law), and with it likewise the law of an intelligible world, to which speculative reason could only point, but could not define its conception. 3. What speculative reason was able to think, but was obliged to leave undetermined as a mere transcendental *ideal,* viz. the *theological* conception of the First Being, to this it gives significance (in a practical view, that is, as a condition of the possibility of the object of a will determined by that law), namely, as the supreme principle of the *summum bonum* in an intelligible world, by means of moral legislation in it invested with sovereign power.

Is our knowledge, however, actually extended in this way by pure practical reason, and is that *immanent* in practical reason which for the speculative was only *transcendent?* Certainly, but *only in a practical point of view.* For we do not thereby take knowledge of the nature of our souls, nor of the intelligible world, nor of the Supreme Being, with respect to what they are in themselves, but we have merely combined the conceptions of them in the *practical* concept of the *summum bonum* as the object of our will, and this altogether *à priori,* but only by means of the moral law, and merely in reference to it, in respect of the object which it commands. But how freedom is possible, and how we are to conceive this kind of causality theoretically and positively, is not thereby discovered; but only that there is such a causality is postulated by the moral law and in its behoof. It is the same with the remaining ideas, the possibility of which no human intelligence will ever fathom, but the truth of which, on the other hand, no sophistry will ever wrest from the conviction even of the commonest man.

VII.—*How is it possible to conceive an extension of Pure Reason in a Practical point of view, without its Knowledge as Speculative being enlarged at the same time?*

In order not to be too abstract, we will answer this question at once in its application to the present case. In order to extend a pure cognition *practically,* there must be an *à priori purpose* given, that is, an end as object (of the will), which independently on all theological principle is presented as practically necessary by an imperative which determines the will directly (a categorical imperative), and in this case that is the *summum bonum*. This, however, is not possible without presupposing three theoretical conceptions (for which, because they are mere conceptions of pure reason, no corresponding intuition can be found, nor consequently by the path of theory any objective reality), namely, freedom, immortality, and God. Thus by the practical law which commands the existence of the highest good possible in a world, the possibility of those objects of pure speculative reason is postulated, and the objective reality which the latter could not assure them. By this the theoretical knowledge of pure reason does indeed obtain an accession; but it consists only in this, that those concepts which otherwise it had to look upon as problematical (merely thinkable) concepts, are now shown assertorially to be such as actually have objects; because practical reason indispensably requires their existence for the possibility of its object, the *summum bonum*, which practically is absolutely necessary, and this justifies theoretical reason in assuming them. But this extension of theoretical reason is no extension of speculative, that is, we cannot make any positive use of it in a *theoretical point of view*. For as nothing is accomplished in this by practical reason, further than that these concepts are real and actually have their (possible) objects, and nothing in the way of intuition of them is given thereby (which indeed could not be demanded), hence the admission of this reality does not render any synthetical proposition possible. Consequently this discovery does not in the least help us to extend this knowledge of ours in a speculative point of view, although it does in respect of the practical employment of pure reason. The above three ideas of speculative reason are still in themselves not cognitions; they are, however, (transcendent) *thoughts* in which there is nothing impossible. Now, by help of an apodictic practical law, being necessary conditions of that which it commands *to be made an object*, they acquire objective reality: that is, we learn from it *that they have objects*, without being able to point out how the conception of them is related to an object, and this, too, is still not a cognition of *these objects*; for we cannot thereby form any synthetical judgment about them, nor determine their application theoretically; consequently we can make no theoretical rational use of them at all, in which use all speculative knowledge of reason consists. Nevertheless, the theoretical knowledge, *not indeed of these objects*, but of reason generally, is so far enlarged by this, that by the practical postulates *objects were given* to those ideas, a merely problematical thought having by this means first acquired objective reality. There is therefore no extension of the knowledge *of given supersensible objects*, but an extension of theoretical reason and of its knowledge in respect of the supersensible generally; inasmuch as it is compelled to admit *that there are such objects*, although it is not able to define them more closely, so as itself to extend this knowledge of the objects (which have now been given it on practical grounds, and only for practical use). For this accession, then, pure theoretical reason, for which all those ideas are transcendent and without object, has simply to thank its practical faculty. In this they become *immanent and constitutive*, being the source of the possibility of *realizing the necessary object* of pure practical reason (the *summum bonum*); whereas apart from this they are transcendent, and merely *regulative* principles of speculative reason, which do not require it to assume a new object beyond experience, but only to bring its use in experience nearer to completeness. But when once reason is in possession of this accession, it will go to work with these ideas as speculative reason (properly only to assure the certainty of its practical use) in a negative manner: that is, not extending but clearing up its knowledge so as on one side to keep off *anthropomorphism*, as the source of *superstition*, or seeming extension of these conceptions by supposed experience; and on the other side *fanaticism*, which promises the same by means of supersensible intuition or feelings of the like kind. All these are hindrances to the practical use of pure reason, so that the removal of them may certainly be considered an extension of our knowledge in a practical point of view, without contradicting the admission that for speculative purposes reason has not in the least gained by this.

Every employment of reason in respect of an object requires pure concepts of the understanding (*categories*), without which no object can be conceived. These can be applied to the theoretical employment of reason, *i.e.*, to that kind of knowledge, only in case an intuition (which is always sensible) is taken as a basis, and therefore merely in order to conceive by means of them an object of possible experience. Now here what have to be thought by means of the categories, in order to be known, are *ideas* of reason, which cannot be given in any experience. Only we are not here concerned with the theoretical knowledge of the objects of these ideas, but only with this, whether they have objects at all. This reality is supplied by pure practical reason, and theoretical reason has nothing further to do in this but to *think* those objects by means of categories. This, as we have elsewhere clearly shown, can be done well enough without needing any intuition (either sensible or supersensible), because the categories have their seat and origin in the pure understanding, simply as the faculty of thought, before and independently on any intuition, and they always only signify an object in general, *no matter in what way it may be given to us.* Now when the categories are to be applied to these ideas, it is not possible to give them any object in intuition; but *that such an object actually exists*, and consequently that the category as a mere form of thought is here not empty but has significance, this is sufficiently assured them by an object which practical reason presents beyond doubt in the concept of the *summum bonum*, namely, the *reality of the conceptions* which are required for the possibility of the *summum bonum*, without, however, effecting by this accession the least extension of our knowledge on theoretical principles.

When these ideas of God, of an intelligible world (the kingdom of God), and of immortality are further determined by predicates taken from our own nature, we must not regard this determination as a *sensualizing* of those pure rational ideas (anthropomorphism), nor as a transcendent knowledge of *supersensible* objects;

for these predicates are no others than understanding and will, considered too in the relation to each other in which they must be conceived in the moral law, and therefore only so far as a pure practical use is made of them. As to all the rest that belongs to these conceptions psychologically, that is, so far as we observe these faculties of ours empirically *in their exercise* (e.g. that the understanding of man is discursive, and its notions therefore not intuitions but thoughts, that these follow one another in time, that his will has its satisfaction always dependent on the existence of its object, &c., which cannot be the case in the Supreme Being), from all this we abstract in that case, and then there remains of the notions by which we conceive a pure intelligence nothing more than just what is required for the possibility of conceiving a moral law. There is then a knowledge of God indeed, but only for practical purposes; and if we attempt to extend it to a theoretical knowledge, we find an understanding that has *intuitions*, not thoughts, a will that is directed to objects on the existence of which its satisfaction does not in the least depend (not to mention the transcendental predicates, as, for example, a magnitude of existence, that is duration, which, however, is not in time, the only possible means we have of conceiving existence as magnitude). Now these are all attributes of which we can form no conception that would help to the *knowledge* of the object, and we learn from this that they can never be used for a *theory* of supersensible beings, so that on this side they are quite incapable of being the foundation of a speculative knowledge, and their use is limited simply to the practice of the moral law.

This last is so obvious, and can be proved so clearly by fact, that we may confidently challenge all pretended *natural theologians* (a singular name)[9] to specify (over and above the merely ontological predicates) one single attribute, whether of the understanding or of the will, determining this object of theirs, of which we could not show incontrovertibly that if we abstract from it everything anthropomorphic, nothing would remain to us but the mere word, without our being able to connect with it the smallest notion by which we could hope for an extension of theoretical knowledge. But as to the practical, there still remains to us of the attributes of understanding and will the conception of a relation to which objective reality is given by the practical law (which determines *à priori* precisely this relation of the understanding to the will). When once this is done, then reality is given to the conception of the object of a will morally determined (the conception of the *summum bonum*), and with it to the conditions of its possibility, the ideas of God, freedom, and immortality, but always only relatively to the practice of the moral law (and not for any speculative purpose).

According to these remarks it is now easy to find the answer to the weighty question: *whether the notion of God is one belonging to Physics* (and therefore also to Metaphysics, which contains the pure *à priori* principles of the former in their universal import) *or to morals*. If we have recourse to God as the Author of all things, in order to *explain* the arrangements of nature or its changes, this is at least not a physical explanation, and is a complete confession that our philosophy has come to an end, since we are obliged to assume something of which in itself we have otherwise no conception, in order to be able to frame a conception of the possibility of what we see before our eyes. Metaphysics, however, cannot enable us to attain *by certain inference* from the knowledge of *this* world to the conception of God and to the proof of His existence, for this reason, that in order to say that this world could be produced only by a God (according to the conception implied by this word) we should know this world as the most perfect whole possible; and for this purpose should also know all possible worlds (in order to be able to compare them with this); in other words, we should be omniscient. It is absolutely impossible, however, to know the existence of this Being from mere concepts, because every existential proposition, that is, every proposition that affirms the existence of a being of which I frame a concept, is a synthetic proposition, that is, one by which I go beyond that conception and affirm of it more than was thought in the conception itself, namely, that this concept *in the understanding* has an object corresponding to it *outside the understanding*, and this it is obviously impossible to elicit by any reasoning. There remains, therefore, only one single process possible for reason to attain this knowledge, namely to start from the supreme principle of its pure practical use (which in every case is directed simply to the *existence* of something as a consequence of reason), and thus determine its object. Then its inevitable problem, namely, the necessary direction of the will to the *summum bonum*, discovers to us not only the necessity of assuming such a First Being in reference to the possibility of this good in the world, but what is most remarkable, something which reason in its progress on the path of physical nature altogether failed to find, namely, an accurately defined conception of this First Being. As we can know only a small part of this world, and can still less compare it with all possible worlds, we may indeed from its order, design, and greatness, infer a wise, good, powerful, &c., Author of it, but not that He is all-wise, all-good, all-powerful, &c. It may indeed, very well be granted that we should be justified in supplying this inevitable defect by a legitimate and reasonable hypothesis, namely, that when wisdom, goodness, &c., are displayed in all the parts that offer themselves to our nearer knowledge, it is just the same in all the rest, and that it would therefore be reasonable to ascribe all possible perfections to the Author of the world; but these are not strict *logical inferences* in which we can pride ourselves on our insight, but only permitted conclusions in which we may be indulged, and which require further recommendation before we can make use of them. On the path of empirical inquiry then (physics) the conception of God remains always a conception of the perfection of the First Being not accurately enough determined to be held adequate to the conception of Deity. (With metaphysic in its transcendental part nothing whatever can be accomplished.)

When I now try to test this conception by reference to the object of practical reason, I find that the moral principle admits as possible only the conception of an Author of the world possessed *of the highest perfection*. He must be *omniscient*, in order to know my conduct up to the inmost root of my mental state in all possible cases and into all future time, *omnipotent,* in order to allot to it its fitting consequences; similarly He must be *omnipresent, eternal,* &c. Thus the moral law, by means of the conception of the *summum bonum* as the object of a pure practical reason, determines the concept of the First Being *as the Supreme Being;* a thing which the physical (and in its higher development the metaphysical), in other words, the whole speculative course of reason, was unable to effect. The conception of God, then, is one that belongs originally not to physics, *i.e.* to speculative reason, but to morals. The same may be said of the other conceptions of reason of which we have treated above as postulates of it in its practical use.

In the history of Grecian philosophy we find no distinct traces of a pure rational theology earlier than *Anaxagoras*; but this is not because the older philosophers had not intelligence or penetration enough to raise themselves to it by the path of speculation, at least with the aid of a thoroughly reasonable hypothesis. What could have been easier, what more natural, than the thought which of itself occurs to everyone, to assume instead of several causes of the world, instead of an indeterminate degree of perfection, a single rational cause having *all perfection?* But the evils in the world seemed to them to be much too serious objections to allow them to feel themselves justified in such a hypothesis. They showed intelligence and penetration then in this very point, that they did not allow themselves to adopt it, but on the contrary looked about amongst natural causes to see if they could not find in them the qualities and power required for a First Being. But when this acute people had advanced so far in their investigations of nature as to treat even moral questions philosophically, on which other nations had never done anything but talk, then first they found a new and practical want, which did not fail to give definiteness to their conception of the First Being: and in this the speculative reason played the part of spectator, or at best had the merit of embellishing a conception that had not grown on its own ground, and of applying a series of confirmations from the study of nature now brought forward for the first time, not indeed to strengthen the authority of this conception (which was already established), but rather to make a show with a supposed discovery of theoretical reason.

From these remarks the reader of the Critique of Pure Speculative Reason will be thoroughly convinced how highly necessary that laborious *deduction* of the categories was, and how fruitful for theology and morals. For if, on the one hand, we place them in the pure understanding, it is by this deduction alone that we can be prevented from regarding them, with *Plato*, as innate, and founding on them extravagant pretensions to theories of the supersensible, to which we can see no end, and by which we should make theology a magic lantern of chimeras: on the other hand, if we regard them as acquired, this deduction saves us from restricting, with *Epicurus*, all and every use of them, even for practical purposes, to the objects and motives of the senses. But now that the Critique has shown by that deduction, *first*, that they are not of empirical origin, but have their seat and source *à priori* in the pure understanding; *secondly*, that as they refer *to objects in general* independently on the intuition of them, hence, although they cannot effect *theoretical knowledge*, except in application to *empirical* objects, yet when applied to an object given by pure practical reason they enable us to *conceive the supersensible* definitely, only so far, however, as it is defined by such predicates as are necessarily connected with the pure *practical purpose* given *à priori* and with its possibility. The speculative restriction of pure reason and its practical extension bring it into that *relation of equality* in which reason in general can be employed suitably to its end, and this example proves better than any other that the path to *wisdom*, if it is to be made sure and not to be impassable or misleading, must with us men inevitably pass through science; but it is not till this is completed that we can be convinced that it leads to this goal.

VIII.—*Of Belief from a Requirement of Pure Reason*

A want or requirement of pure reason in its speculative use leads only to a *hypothesis*; that of pure practical reason to a *postulate*; for in the former case I ascend from the result as high as I please in the series of causes, not in order to give objective reality to the result (*e.g.* the causal connexion of things and changes in the world), but in order thoroughly to satisfy my inquiring reason in respect of it. Thus I see before me order and design in nature, and need not resort to speculation to assure myself of their *reality*, but to *explain* them I have *to pre-suppose a Deity* as their cause; and then since the inference from an effect to a definite cause is always uncertain and doubtful, especially to a cause so precise and so perfectly defined as we have to conceive in God, hence the highest degree of certainty to which this pre-supposition can be brought is, that it is the most rational opinion for us men[10]. On the other hand, a requirement of pure *practical* reason is based on a *duty*, that of making something (the *summum bonum*) the object of my will so as to promote it with all my powers; in which case I must suppose its possibility, and consequently also the conditions necessary thereto, namely, God, freedom, and immortality; since I cannot prove these by my speculative reason, although neither can I refute them. This duty is founded on something that is indeed quite independent on these suppositions, and is of itself apodictically certain, namely, the moral law; and so far it needs no further support by theoretical views as to the inner constitution of things, the secret final aim of the order of the world, or a presiding ruler thereof, in order to bind me in the most perfect manner to act in unconditional conformity to the law. But the subjective effect of this law, namely, the mental *disposition* conformed to it and made necessary by it, to promote the practically possible *summum bonum*, this pre-supposes at least that the latter is *possible*, for it would be practically impossible to strive after the object of a conception which at bottom was empty and had no object. Now the above-mentioned postulates concern only the physical or metaphysical conditions of the *possibility* of the *summum bonum*; in a word, those which lie in the nature of things; not, however, for the sake of an arbitrary speculative purpose, but of a practically necessary end of a pure rational will, which in this case does not *choose*, but *obeys* an inexorable command of reason, the foundation of which is *objective*, in the constitution of things as they must be universally judged by pure reason, and is not based on *inclination*; for we are in nowise justified in assuming, on account of what we *wish* on merely *subjective* grounds, that the means thereto are possible or that its object is real. This, then, is an absolutely necessary requirement, and what it pre-supposes is not merely justified as an allowable hypothesis, but as a postulate in a practical point of view; and admitting that the pure moral law inexorably binds every man as a command (not as a rule of prudence), the righteous man may say: I *will* that there be a God, that my existence in this world be also an existence outside the chain of physical causes, and in a pure world of the understanding, and lastly, that my duration be endless; I firmly abide by this, and will not let this faith be taken from me; for in this instance alone my interest, because I *must* not relax anything of it, inevitably determines my judgment, without regarding sophistries, however unable I may be to answer them or to oppose them with others more plausible.[12]

In order to prevent misconception in the use of a notion as yet so unusual as that of a faith of pure practical reason, let me be permitted to add one more remark. It might almost seem as if this rational faith were here announced as itself a *command*, namely, that we should assume the *summum bonum* as possible. But a faith that is commanded is nonsense. Let the preceding analysis, however, be remembered of what is required to be supposed in the conception of the *summum bonum*, and it will be seen that it cannot be commanded to assume this possibility, and no practical disposition of mind is required to *admit* it; but that speculative reason must concede it without being asked, for no one can affirm that it is *impossible* in itself that rational beings in the world should at the same time be worthy of happiness in conformity with the moral law, and also possess this happiness proportionately. Now in respect of the first element of the *summum bonum*, namely, that which concerns morality, the moral law gives merely a command, and to doubt the possibility of that element would be the same as to call in question the moral law itself. But as regards the second element of that object, namely, happiness perfectly proportioned to that worthiness, it is true that there is no need of a command to admit its possibility in general, for theoretical reason has nothing to say against it; but *the manner* in which we have to conceive this harmony of the laws of nature with those of freedom has in it something in respect of which we have a *choice*, because theoretical reason decides nothing with apodictic certainty about it, and in respect of this there may be a moral interest which turns the scale.

I had said above that in a mere course of nature in the world an accurate correspondence between happiness and moral worth is not to be expected, and must be regarded as impossible, and that therefore the possibility of the *summum bonum* cannot be admitted from this side except on the supposition of a moral Author of the world. I purposely reserved the restriction of this judgment to the *subjective* conditions of our reason, in order not to make use of it until the manner of this belief should be defined more precisely. The fact is that the impossibility referred to is *merely subjective*, that is, our reason finds it *impossible for it* to render conceivable in the way of a mere course of nature a connexion so exactly proportioned and so thoroughly adapted to an end, between two sets of events happening according to such distinct laws; although, as with everything else in nature that is adapted to an end, it cannot prove, that is, show by sufficient objective reasons, that it is not possible by universal laws of nature.

Now, however, a deciding principle of a different kind comes into play to turn the scale in this uncertainty of speculative reason. The command to promote the *summum bonum* is established on an objective basis (in practical reason); the possibility of the same in general is likewise established on an objective basis (in theoretical reason, which has nothing to say against it). But reason cannot decide objectively in what way we are to conceive this possibility; whether by universal laws of nature without a wise Author presiding over nature, or only on supposition of such an Author. Now here there comes in a *subjective* condition of reason the only way theoretically possible for it, of conceiving the exact harmony of the kingdom of nature with the kingdom of morals, which is the condition of the possibility of the *summum bonum*; and at the same time the only one conducive to morality (which depends on an objective law of reason). Now since the promotion of this *summum bonum*, and therefore the supposition of its possibility, are *objectively* necessary (though only as a result of practical reason), while at the same time the manner in which we would conceive it rests with our own choice, and in this choice a free interest of pure practical reason decides for the assumption of a wise Author of the world; it is clear that the principle that herein determines our judgment, though as a want it is *subjective*, yet at the same time being the means of promoting what is *objectively* (practically) necessary, is the foundation of a *maxim* of belief in a moral point of view, that is, a *faith of pure practical reason*. This, then, is not commanded, but being a voluntary determination of our judgment, conducive to the moral (commanded) purpose, and moreover harmonizing with the theoretical requirement of reason, to assume that existence and to make it the foundation of our further employment of reason, it has itself sprung from the moral disposition of mind; it may therefore at times waver even in the well-disposed, but can never be reduced to unbelief.

IX.—*Of the Wise Adaptation of Man's Cognitive Faculties to his Practical Destination*

If human nature is destined to endeavour after the *summum bonum*, we must suppose also that the measure of its cognitive faculties, and particularly their relation to one another, is suitable to this end. Now the Critique of Pure *Speculative* Reason proves that this is incapable of solving satisfactorily the most weighty problems that are proposed to it, although it does not ignore the natural and important hints received from the same reason, nor the great steps that it can make to approach to this great goal that is set before it, which, however, it can never reach of itself, even with the help of the greatest knowledge of nature. Nature then seems here to have provided us only in a *step-motherly* fashion with the faculty required for our end.

Suppose now that in this matter nature had conformed to our wish, and had given us that capacity of discernment or that enlightenment which we would gladly possess, or which some *imagine* they actually possess, what would in all probability be the consequence? Unless our whole nature were at the same time changed, our inclinations, which always have the first word, would first of all demand their own satisfaction, and, joined with rational reflection, the greatest possible and most lasting satisfaction, under the name of happiness; the moral law would afterwards speak, in order to keep them within their proper bounds, and even to subject them all to a higher end, which has no regard to inclination. But instead of the conflict that the moral disposition has now to carry on with the inclinations, in which, though after some defeats, moral strength of mind may be gradually acquired, *God* and *eternity* with their *awful majesty* would stand unceasingly *before our eyes* (for what we can prove perfectly is to us as certain as that of which we are assured by the sight of our eyes). Transgression of the law, would, no doubt, be avoided; what is commanded would be done; but the mental *disposition*, from which actions ought to proceed, cannot be infused by any command, and in this case the spur of action is ever active and *external,* so that reason has no need to exert itself in order to gather strength to resist the inclinations by a lively representation of the dignity of the law: hence most of the actions that conformed to the law would be done from fear, a few only from hope, and none at all from duty, and the moral worth of actions, on which alone in the eyes of supreme wisdom the worth of the person and even that of the world depends, would cease to exist. As long as the nature of man remains what it is, his conduct would thus be changed into mere mechanism, in which, as in a puppet-show, everything would *gesticulate* well, but there would be *no life* in the figures. Now, when it is quite otherwise with us, when with all the effort of our reason we have only a very obscure and doubtful view into the future, when the Governor of the world allows us only to conjecture His existence and His majesty, not to behold them or prove them clearly; and, on the other hand, the moral law within us, without promising or threatening anything with certainty, demands of us disinterested respect; and only when this respect has become active and dominant does it allow us by means of it a prospect into the world of the supersensible, and then only with weak glances; all this being so, there is room for true moral disposition, immediately devoted to the law, and a rational creature can become worthy of sharing in the *summum bonum* that corresponds to the worth of his person and not merely to his actions. Thus what the study of nature and of man teaches us sufficiently elsewhere may well be true here also; that the unsearchable wisdom by which we exist is not less worthy of admiration in what it has denied than in what it has granted.

PART SECOND

METHODOLOGY OF PURE
PRACTICAL REASON

METHODOLOGY
OF PURE PRACTICAL REASON

BY the *methodology* of pure *practical* reason we are not to understand the mode of proceeding with pure practical principles
(whether in study or in exposition), with a view to a scientific
knowledge of them, which alone is what is properly called method
elsewhere in *theoretical* philosophy (for popular knowledge
requires a *manner*, science a *method*, i.e. a process *according to principles of reason* by which alone the manifold of any branch of knowledge can become a *system*). On the contrary, by this methodology
is understood the mode in which[1] we can give the laws of pure
practical reason *access* to the human mind, and *influence* on its
maxims, that is, by which we can make the objectively practical
reason *subjectively* practical also.

Now it is clear enough that those determining principles of the
will which alone make maxims properly moral and give them a
moral worth, namely, the direct conception of the law and the
objective necessity of obeying it as our duty, must be regarded as
the proper springs of action, since otherwise *legality* of actions
might be produced, but not *morality* of character. But it is not so
clear: on the contrary, it must at first sight seem to everyone very
improbable that, even subjectively, that exhibition of pure virtue
can have *more power* over the human mind, and supply a far
stronger spring even for affecting that legality of actions, and can

produce more powerful resolutions to prefer the law, from pure respect for it, to every other consideration, than all the deceptive allurements of pleasure or of all that may be reckoned as happiness, or even than all threatenings of pain and misfortune. Nevertheless, this is actually the case, and if human nature were not so constituted, no mode of presenting the law by roundabout ways and indirect recommendations would ever produce morality of character. All would be simple hypocrisy; the law would be hated, or at least despised, while it was followed for the sake of one's own advantage. The letter of the law (legality) would be found in our actions, but not the spirit of it in our minds (morality); and as with all our efforts we could not quite free ourselves from reason in our judgment, we must inevitably appear in our own eyes worthless, depraved men, even though we should seek to compensate ourselves for this mortification before the inner tribunal, by enjoying the pleasure that a supposed natural or divine law might be imagined to have connected with it a sort of police machinery, regulating its operations by what was done without troubling itself about the motives for doing it.

It cannot indeed be denied that in order to bring an uncultivated or degraded mind into the track of moral goodness some preparatory guidance is necessary, to attract it by a view of its own advantage, or to alarm it by fear of loss; but as soon as this mechanical work, these leading-strings, have produced some effect, then we must bring before the mind the pure moral motive, which, not only because it is the only one that can be the foundation of a character (a practically consistent habit of mind with unchangeable maxims), but also because it teaches a man to feel his own dignity, gives the mind a power unexpected even by himself, to tear himself from all sensible attachments so far as they would fain have the rule, and to find a rich compensation for the sacrifice he offers, in the independence of his rational nature and the greatness of soul to which he sees that he is destined. We will therefore show, by such observations as every one can make, that this property of our minds, this receptivity for a pure moral interest, and consequently the moving force of the pure conception of virtue, when it is properly applied to the human heart, is the most powerful spring, and, when a continued and punctual observance of moral maxims is in question, the only spring of good conduct. It must, however, be remembered that if these observations only prove the reality of such a feeling, but do not show any moral improvement brought about by it, this is no argument against the only method that exists of making the objectively practical laws of pure reason subjectively practical, through the mere force of the conception of duty; nor does it prove that this method is a vain delusion. For as it has never yet come into vogue, experience can say nothing of its results; one can only ask for proofs of the receptivity for such springs, and these I will now briefly present, and then sketch the method of founding and cultivating genuine moral dispositions.

When we attend to the course of conversation in mixed companies, consisting not merely of learned persons and subtle reasoners, but also of men of business or of women, we observe that, besides story-telling and jesting, another kind of entertainment finds a place in them, namely, argument; for stories, if they are to have novelty and interest, are soon exhausted, and jesting is likely to become insipid. Now of all argument there is none in which persons are more ready to join who find any other subtle discussion tedious, none that brings more liveliness into the company, than that which concerns the *moral worth* of this or that action by which the character of some person is to be made out. Persons, to whom in other cases anything subtle and speculative in theoretical questions is dry and irksome, presently join in when the question is to make out the moral import of a good or bad action that has been related, and they display an exactness, a refinement, a subtlety, in excogitating everything that can lessen the purity of purpose, and consequently the degree of virtue in it, which we do not expect from them in any other kind of speculation. In these criticisms persons who are passing judgment on others often reveal their own character: some, in exercising their judicial office, especially upon the dead, seem inclined chiefly to defend the goodness that is related of this or that deed against all injurious charges of insincerity, and ultimately to defend the whole moral worth of the person against the reproach of dissimulation and secret wickedness; others, on the contrary, turn their thoughts more upon attacking this worth by accusation and fault-finding. We cannot always, however, attribute to these latter the intention of arguing away virtue altogether out of all human examples in order to make it an empty name: often, on the contrary, it is only well-meant strictness in determining the true moral import of actions according to an uncompromising law. Comparison with such a law, instead of with examples, lowers self-conceit in moral matters very much, and not merely teaches humility, but makes everyone feel it when he examines himself closely. Nevertheless, we can for the most part observe in those who defend the purity of purpose in given examples, that where there is the presumption of upright-ness they are anxious to remove even the least spot, lest, if all exam-ples had their truthfulness disputed, and if the purity of all human virtue were denied, it might in the end be regarded as a mere phantom, and so all effort to attain it be made light of as vain affec-tation and delusive conceit.

I do not know why the educators of youth have not long since made use of this propensity of reason to enter with pleasure upon the most subtle examination of the practical questions that are thrown up; and why they have not, after first laying the foundation of a purely moral catechism, searched through the biographies of ancient and modern times with the view of having at hand instances of the duties laid down, in which, especially by compari-son of similar actions under different circumstances, they might exercise the critical judgment of their scholars in remarking their greater or less moral significance. This is a thing in which they would find that even early youth, which is still unripe for specula-tion of other kinds, would soon become very acute and not a little interested, because it feels the progress of its faculty of judgment; and what is most important, they could hope with confidence that the frequent practice of knowing and approving good conduct in all its purity, and on the other hand of remarking with regret or contempt the least deviation from it, although it may be pursued only as a sport in which children may compete with one another, yet will leave a lasting impression of esteem on the one hand and disgust on the other; and so, by the mere habit of looking on such actions as deserving approval or blame, a good foundation would be laid for uprightness in the future course of life. Only I wish they would spare them the example of so-called *noble* (super-meritorious) actions in which our sentimental books so much abound, and would refer all to duty merely, and to the worth that a man can and must give himself in his own eyes by the consciousness of not having transgressed it, since whatever runs up into empty wishes and longings after inaccessible perfection produces mere heroes of romance, who, while they pique themselves on their feeling for transcendent greatness, release themselves in return from the observance of common and every-day obligations, which then seem to them petty and insignificant.[2]

But if it is asked, what then is really *pure* morality, by which as a touchstone we must test the moral significance of every action, then I must admit that it is only philosophers that can make the decision of this question doubtful, for to common sense it has been decided long ago, not indeed by abstract general formulæ, but by habitual use, like the distinction between the right and left hand. We will then point out the criterion of pure virtue in an example first, and imagining that it is set before a boy of, say, ten years old, for his judgment, we will see whether he would necessarily judge so of himself without being guided by his teacher. Tell him the history of an honest man whom men want to persuade to join the calumniators of an innocent and powerless person (say, Anne Boleyn, accused by Henry VIII of England). He is offered advantages, great gifts, or high rank; he rejects them. This will excite mere approbation and applause in the mind of the hearer. Now begins the threatening of loss. Amongst these traducers are his best friends, who now renounce his friendship; near kinsfolk, who threaten to disinherit him (he being without fortune): powerful persons, who can persecute and harass him in all places and circumstances; a prince who threatens him with loss of freedom, yea, loss of life. Then to fill the measure of suffering, and that he may feel the pain that only the morally good heart can feel very deeply, let us conceive his family threatened with extreme distress and want, *entreating him to yield*; conceive himself, though upright, yet with feelings not hard or insensible either to compassion or to his own distress; conceive him, I say, at the moment when he wishes that he had never lived to see the day that exposed him to such unutterable anguish, yet remaining true to his uprightness of purpose, without wavering or even doubting; then will my youthful hearer be raised gradually from mere approval to admiration, from that to amazement, and finally to the greatest veneration, and a lively wish that he himself could be such a man (though certainly not in such circumstances). Yet virtue is here worth so much only because it costs so much, not because it brings any profit. All the admiration, and even the endeavour to resemble this character, rest wholly on the purity of the moral principle, which can only be strikingly shown by removing from the springs of action everything that men may regard as part of happiness. Morality then must have the more power over the human heart the more purely it is exhibited. Whence it follows that if the law of morality and the image of holiness and virtue are to exercise any influence at all on our souls, they can do so only so far as they are laid to heart in their purity as motives, unmixed with any view to prosperity, for it is in suffering that they display themselves most nobly. Now that whose removal strengthens the effect of a moving force must have been a hindrance, consequently every admixture of motives taken from our own happiness is a hindrance to the influence of the moral law on the heart. I affirm further, that even in that admired action, if the motive from which it was done was a high regard for duty, then it is just this respect for the law that has the greatest influence on the mind of the spectator, not any pretension to a supposed inward greatness of mind or noble meritorious sentiments; consequently duty, not merit, must have not only the most definite, but, when it is represented in the true light of its inviolability, the most penetrating influence on the mind.

It is more necessary than ever to direct attention to this method in our times, when men hope to produce more effect on the mind with soft, tender feelings, or high-flown, puffing-up pretensions, which rather wither the heart than strengthen it, than by a plain and earnest representation of duty, which is more suited to human imperfection and to progress in goodness. To set before children, as a pattern, actions that are called noble, magnanimous, meritorious, with the notion of captivating them by infusing an enthusiasm for such actions, is to defeat our end. For as they are still so backward in the observance of the commonest duty, and even in the correct estimation of it, this means simply to make them fantastical romancers betimes. But, even with the instructed and experienced part of mankind, this supposed spring has, if not an injurious, at least no genuine moral effect on the heart, which, however, is what it was desired to produce.

All *feelings*, especially those that are to produce unwonted exertions, must accomplish their effect at the moment they are at their height, and before they calm down; otherwise they effect nothing; for as there was nothing to strengthen the heart, but only to excite it, it naturally returns to its normal moderate tone, and thus falls back into its previous languor. *Principles* must be built on conceptions; on any other basis there can only be paroxysms, which can give the person no moral worth, nay, not even confidence in himself, without which the highest good in man, consciousness of the morality of his mind and character, cannot exist. Now if these conceptions are to become subjectively practical, we must not rest satisfied with admiring the objective law of morality, and esteeming it highly in reference to humanity, but we must consider the conception of it in relation to man as an individual, and then this law appears in a form indeed that is highly deserving of respect, but not so pleasant as if it belonged to the element to which he is naturally accustomed, but, on the contrary, as often compelling him to quit this element, not without self-denial, and to betake himself to a higher, in which he can only maintain himself with trouble and with unceasing apprehension of a relapse. In a word, the moral law demands obedience, from duty, not from predilection, which cannot and ought not to be pre-supposed at all.

Let us now see in an example whether the conception of an action as a noble and magnanimous one has more subjective moving power than if the action is conceived merely as duty in relation to the solemn law of morality. The action by which a man endeavours at the greatest peril of life to rescue people from shipwreck, at last losing his life in the attempt, is reckoned on one side as duty, but on the other and for the most part as a meritorious action, but our esteem for it is much weakened by the notion of *duty to himself,* which seems in this case to be somewhat infringed. More decisive is the magnanimous sacrifice of life for the safety of one's country; and yet there still remains some scruple whether it is a perfect duty to devote one's self to this purpose spontaneously and unbidden, and the action has not in itself the full force of a pattern and impulse to imitation. But if an indispensable duty be in question, the transgression of which violates the moral law itself, and without regard to the welfare of mankind, and as it were tramples on its holiness (such as are usually called duties to God, because in Him we conceive the ideal of holiness in substance), then we give our most perfect esteem to the pursuit of it at the sacrifice of all that can have any value for the dearest inclinations, and we find our soul strengthened and elevated by such an example, when we convince ourselves by contemplation of it that human nature is capable of so great an elevation above every motive that nature can oppose to it. Juvenal describes such an example in a climax which makes the reader feel vividly the force of the spring that is contained in the pure law of duty, as duty:

> Esto bonus miles, tutor bonus, arbiter idem
> Integer; ambiguae si quando citabere testis
> Incertaeque rei, Phalaris licet imperet ut sis

Falsus, et admoto dictet periuria tauro,
Summum crede nefas animam praeferre pudori,
Et propter vitam vivendi perdere causas.

When we can bring any flattering thought of merit into our action, then the motive is already somewhat alloyed with self-love, and has therefore some assistance from the side of the sensibility. But to postpone everything to the holiness of duty alone, and to be conscious that we *can* because our own reason recognizes this as its command and says that we *ought* to do it, this is, as it were, to raise ourselves altogether above the world of sense, and there is inseparably involved in the same a consciousness of the law, as a spring of a faculty *that controls the sensibility*; and although this is not always attended with effect, yet frequent engagement with this spring, and the at first minor attempts at using it, give hope that this effect may be wrought, and that by degrees the greatest, and that a purely moral interest in it may be produced in us.

The method then takes the following course. At first we are only concerned to make the judging of actions by moral laws a natural employment accompanying all our own free actions as well as the observation of those of others, and to make it, as it were, a habit, and to sharpen this judgment, asking first whether the action *conforms* objectively *to the moral law*, and to what law; and we distinguish the law that merely furnishes a *principle* of obligation from that which is really *obligatory* (*leges obligandi a legibus obligantibus*); as, for instance, the law of what men's *wants* require from me, as contrasted with that which their *rights* demand, the latter of which prescribes essential, the former only non-essential duties; and thus we teach how to distinguish different kinds of duties which meet in the same action. The other point to which attention must be directed is the question whether the action was also (subjectively) done *for the sake of the moral law*, so that it not only is morally correct as a deed, but also, by the maxim from which it is done, has moral worth as a disposition. Now there is no doubt that this practice, and the resulting culture of our reason in judging merely of the practical, must gradually produce a certain interest even in the law of reason, and consequently in morally good actions. For we ultimately take a liking for a thing, the contemplation of which makes us feel that the use of our cognitive faculties is extended, and this extension is especially furthered by that in which we find moral correctness, since it is only in such an order of things that reason, with its faculty of determining *à priori* on principle what ought to be done, can find satisfaction. An observer of nature takes liking at last to objects that at first offended his senses, when he discovers in them the great adaptation of their organization to design, so that his reason finds food in its contemplation. So Leibnitz spared an insect that he had carefully examined with the microscope, and replaced it on its leaf, because he had found himself instructed by the view of it, and had as it were received a benefit from it.

But this employment of the faculty of judgment, which makes us feel our own cognitive powers, is not yet the interest in actions and in their morality itself. It merely causes us to take pleasure in engaging in such criticism, and it gives to virtue or the disposition that conforms to moral laws a form of beauty, which is admired, but not on that account sought after (*laudatur et alget*); as everything the contemplation of which produces a consciousness of the harmony of our powers of conception, and in which we feel the whole of our faculty of knowledge (understanding and imagination) strengthened, produces a satisfaction, which may also be communicated to others, while nevertheless the existence of the object remains indifferent to us, being only regarded as the occasion of our becoming aware of the capacities in us which are elevated above mere animal nature. Now however, the *second* exercise comes in, the living exhibition of morality of character by examples, in which attention is directed to purity of will, first only as a negative perfection, in so far as in an action done from duty no motives of inclination have any influence in determining it. By this the pupil's attention is fixed upon the consciousness of his *freedom*, and although this renunciation at first excites a feeling of pain, nevertheless, by its withdrawing the pupil from the constraint of even real wants, there is proclaimed to him at the same time a deliverance from the manifold dissatisfaction in which all these wants entangle him, and the mind is made capable of receiving the sensation of satisfaction from other sources. The heart is freed and lightened of a burden that always secretly presses on it, when instances of pure moral resolutions reveal to the man an inner faculty of which otherwise he has no right knowledge, *the inward freedom* to release himself from the boisterous importunity of inclinations, to such a degree that none of them, not even the dearest, shall have any influence on a resolution, for which we are now to employ our reason. Suppose a case where *I alone* know that the wrong is on my side, and although a free confession of it and the offer of satisfaction are so strongly opposed by vanity selfishness, and even an otherwise not illegitimate antipathy to the man whose rights are impaired by me, I am nevertheless able to discard all these considerations; in this there is implied a consciousness of independence on inclinations and circumstances, and of the possibility of being sufficient for myself, which is salutary to me in general for other purposes also. And now the law of duty, in consequence of the positive worth which obedience to it makes us feel, finds easier access through the *respect for ourselves* in the consciousness of our freedom. When this is well established, when a man dreads nothing more than to find himself, on self-examination, worthless and contemptible in his own eyes, then every good moral disposition can be grafted on it, because this is the best, nay, the only guard that can keep off from the mind the pressure of ignoble and corrupting motives.

I have only intended to point out the most general maxims of the methodology of moral cultivation and exercise. As the manifold variety of duties requires special rules for each kind, and this would be a prolix affair, I shall be readily excused if in a work like this, which is only preliminary, I content myself with these outlines.

CONCLUSION

Two things fill the mind with ever new and increasing admiration and awe, the oftener and the more steadily we reflect on them: *the starry heavens above and the moral law within.* I have not to search for them and conjecture them as though they were veiled in darkness or were in the transcendent region beyond my horizon; I see them before me and connect them directly with the consciousness of my existence. The former begins from the place I occupy in the external world of sense, and enlarges my connexion therein to an unbounded extent with worlds upon worlds and systems of systems, and moreover into limitless times of their periodic motion, its beginning and continuance. The second begins from my invisible self, my personality, and exhibits me in a world which has true infinity, but which is traceable only by the understanding, and with which I discern that I am not in a merely contingent but in a universal and necessary connexion, as I am also thereby with all those visible worlds. The former view of a countless multitude of worlds annihilates, as it were, my importance as an *animal creature,* which after it has been for a short time provided with vital power, one knows not how, must again give back the matter of which it was formed to the planet it inhabits (a mere speck in the universe). The second, on the contrary, infinitely elevates my worth as an *intelligence* by my personality, in which the moral law reveals to me a life independent on animality and even on the whole sensible world— at least so far as may be inferred from the destination assigned to my existence by this law, a destination not restricted to conditions and limits of this life, but reaching into the infinite.

But though admiration and respect may excite to inquiry, they cannot supply the want of it. What, then, is to be done in order to enter on this in a useful manner and one adapted to the loftiness of the subject? Examples may serve in this as a warning, and also for imitation. The contemplation of the world began from the noblest spectacle that the human senses present to us, and that our understanding can bear to follow in their vast reach; and it ended—in astrology. Morality began with the noblest attribute of human nature, the development and cultivation of which give a prospect of infinite utility; and ended—in fanaticism or superstition. So it is with all crude attempts where the principal part of the business depends on the use of reason, a use which does not come of itself, like the use of the feet, by frequent exercise, especially when attributes are in question which cannot be directly exhibited in common experience. But after the maxim had come into vogue, though late, to examine carefully beforehand all the steps that reason purposes to take, and not to let it proceed otherwise than in the track of a previously well-considered method, then the study of the structure of the universe took quite a different direction, and thereby attained an incomparably happier result. The fall of a stone, the motion of a sling, resolved into their elements and the forces that are manifested in them, and treated mathematically, produced at last that clear and henceforward unchangeable insight into the system of the world, which as observation is continued may hope always to extend itself, but need never fear to be compelled to retreat.

This example may suggest to us to enter on the same path in treating of the moral capacities of our nature, and may give us hope of a like good result. We have at hand the instances of the moral judgment of reason. By analysing these into their elementary conceptions, and in default of *mathematics* adopting a process similar to that of *chemistry*, the *separation* of the empirical from the rational elements that may be found in them, by repeated experiments on common sense, we may exhibit both *pure*, and learn with certainty what each part can accomplish of itself, so as to prevent on the one hand the errors of a still *crude* untrained judgment, and on the other hand (what is far more necessary) the *extravagances of genius*, by which, as by the adepts of the philosopher's stone, without any methodical study or knowledge of nature, visionary treasures are promised and the true are thrown away. In one word, science (critically undertaken and methodically directed) is the narrow gate that leads to the true *doctrine of practi-*

cal wisdom,[3] if we understand by this not merely what one ought to *do*, but what ought to serve *teachers* as a guide to construct well and clearly the road to wisdom which everyone should travel, and to secure others from going astray. Philosophy must always continue to be the guardian of this science; and although the public does not take any interest in its subtle investigations, it must take an interest in the resulting *doctrines*, which such an examination first puts in a clear light.

ENDNOTES

BOOK I
CHAPTER I

[¹ Literally, "to have a firm seat in any saddle." It may be noted that Kant's father was a saddler.]

[² Not in the original text.]

³ Propositions which in mathematics or physics are called *practical* ought properly to be called *technical*. For they have nothing to do with the determination of the will; they only point out how a certain effect is to be produced, and are therefore just as theoretical as any propositions which express the connexion of a cause with an effect. Now whoever chooses the effect must also choose the cause.

⁴ [The original sentence is defective; Hartenstein supplies "enthält."]

⁵ [Reading "empfindet" instead of "empfiehlt."]

⁶ [The original text is, I think, corrupt.]

⁷ [The original text has "practical," obviously an error.]

⁸ [By "immanent" Kant means what is strictly confined within the limits of experience; by "transcendent" what pretends to overpass these bounds. Cf. *Kritik der reinen Vernunft*, ed. Rosenkr., p. 240. Meiklejohn's transl., p. 210.]

⁹ [Is a "Verstandeswesen."]

¹⁰ [The original has "practical"; clearly an error.]

¹¹ [The verb, indispensable to the sense, is absent from the original text.]

CHAPTER II

¹ [Or "immediately," *i.e.* without reference to any ulterior result.]

² [The original has "objects" [objecte], which makes no sense. I have therefore ventured to correct it.]

³ Besides this, the expression *sub ratione boni* is also ambiguous. For it may mean: We represent something to ourselves as good, when and because we *desire* (will) it; or, we desire something because we *represent* it to ourselves as

good, so that either the desire determines the notion of the object as good, or the notion of good determines the desire (the will); so that in the first case *sub ratione boni* would mean we will something *under the idea* of the good; in the second, *in consequence of this idea,* which, as determining the volition, must precede it.

⁴ [The English language marks the distinction in question, though not perfectly. "Evil" is not absolutely restricted to moral evil; we speak also of physical evils; but certainly when not so qualified it applies usually (as an adjective, perhaps exclusively) to moral evil. "Bad" is more general; but when used with a word connoting moral qualities, it expresses moral evil; for example, a "bad man," a "bad scholar." These words are etymologically the same as the German "übel" and "böse" respectively. "Good" is ambiguous, being opposed to "bad," as well as to "evil," but the corresponding German word is equally ambiguous.]

⁵ [Rosenkranz' text has "law"—certainly an error ("Gesetz" for 'Gefühl"); Hartenstein corrects it.]

⁶ [For the meaning of this expression, see the *Critique of Pure Reason,* trans. by Meiklejohn, p. 82.]

⁷ [Adopting Hartenstein's conjecture "gemeinste," for "reinste," "purest."]

[⁸ Read "weil" with Hartenstein, not "womit."]

CHAPTER III

¹ We may say of every action that conforms to the law, but is not done for the sake of the law, that it is morally good in the *letter,* not in the *spirit* (the intention).

²["Jener," in Rosenkranz' text is an error. We must read either "jene," "this respect," or "jenes," "this feeling." Hartenstein adopts "jenes."]

³ [The original sentence is incomplete. I have completed it in what seems the simplest way.]

⁴ If we examine accurately the notion of respect for persons as it has been already laid down, we shall perceive that it always rests on the consciousness of a duty which an example shows us, and that respect, therefore, can never have any but a moral ground, and that it is very good and even, in a psychological point of view, very useful for the knowledge of mankind, that whenever we use this expression we should attend to this secret and marvellous, yet often recurring, regard which men in their judgment pay to the moral law.

⁵ This law is in striking contrast with the principle of private happiness which some make the supreme principle of morality. This would be expressed thus: *Love thyself above everything, and God and thy neighbour for thine own sake.*

⁶ [Compare Butler:—"Though we should suppose it impossible for particular affections to be absolutely coincident with the moral principle, and consequently should allow that such creatures . . . would for ever remain defectible; yet their danger of actually deviating from right may be almost infinitely less-

ened, and they fully fortified against what remains of it—if that may be called danger against which there is an adequate effectual security."—*Analogy*, Fitzgerald's Ed., p. 100.]

7 [What renders this discussion not irrelevant is the fact that the German language, like the English, possesses but one word to express φιλεῖν, ἀγαπᾶν, and ἐρᾶν. The first, φιλεῖν, expresses the love of affection. The general good-will due from man to man had no name in classical Greek; it is described in one aspect of it by Aristotle as φιλία ἄνευ πάθους καὶ τοῦ στέργειν (Eth. Nic. iv. 65); elsewhere, however, he calls it simply φιλία (viii. 11, 7). The verb ἀγαπάω was used by the LXX in the precept quoted in the text, though elsewhere they employed it as = ἐρᾶν. But in the New Test. the verb, and with it the noun ἀγάπη (which is not found in classical writers), were appropriated to this state of mind. Aristotle, it may be observed, uses ἀγαπάω, of love to one's own better part (ix. 8, 6). 'Ερᾶν does not occur in the New Test. at all. Butler's Sermons on Love of our Neighbour, and Love of God, may be usefully compared with these observations of Kant.]

8 [Read "denen," not "dem."]

9 [See note on Conscience.]

10 [Reading "aufzugeben."]

11 [Vaucanson constructed an automaton flute-player which imitated accurately the movements and the effects of a genuine performer, and subsequently a mechanical duck which swam, dived, quacked, took barley from the hand, ate, drank, digested, dressed its wings, &c., quite naturally. This was exhibited in Paris in 1741. These automata are described by D'Alembert in the *Encyclopédie*, Arts. *Androïde* and *Automata:* cf. also Condorcet, *Éloges*, tom. i., p. 643, ed. 1847.]

12 [Moses Mendelssohn, a distinguished philosopher, grandfather of the musical composer. He is said to have been the prototype of Lessing's *Nathan der Weise*.]

13 [The original is somewhat ambiguous; it has been suggested that "the former" refers to the Understanding ("Verstand" in "Verstandesbegriff"). I am satisfied that it refers to "Vernunftbegriff," for it is not the Understanding, but the Reason that seeks the unconditioned. Compare *Kritik der R.V.*, p. 262 (326). "The transcendental concept of the reason always aims at absolute totality in the synthesis of the conditions, and never rests except in the absolutely unconditioned." (*Meiklejohn*, p. 228).]

14 [Rosenkranz erroneously reads "unbedingt," "unconditioned"; and "musste" for "müsste."]

BOOK II

CHAPTER II

1 [The original has not *'und,'* but *'als,'* which does not give any satisfactory sense. I have, therefore, adopted Hartenstein's emendation, which seems at least to give the meaning intended.]

2 [See *Preface*, p. 115, *note*.]

3 It seems, nevertheless, impossible for a creature to have the *conviction* of his unwavering firmness of mind in the progress towards goodness. On this account the Christian religion makes it come only from the same Spirit that works sanctification, that is, this firm purpose, and with it the consciousness of steadfastness[4] in the moral progress. But naturally one who is conscious that he has persevered through a long portion of his life up to the end in the progress to the better, and this from genuine moral motives, may well have the comforting hope, though not the certainty, that even in an existence prolonged beyond this life he will continue steadfast in these principles; and although he is never justified here in his own eyes, nor can ever hope to be so in the increased perfection of his nature, to which he looks forward, together with an increase of duties, nevertheless in this progress which, though it is directed to a goal infinitely remote, yet is in God's sight regarded as equivalent to possession, he may have a prospect of a *blessed* future; for this is the word that reason employs to designate perfect *well-being* independent on all contingent causes of the world, and which, like *holiness*, is an idea that can be contained only in an endless progress and its totality, and consequently is never fully attained by a creature.

4 [The ὑπομονή of the N. T.]

5 [The original has "a Supreme Nature." "Natur," however, almost invariably means "physical nature"; therefore Hartenstein supplies the words "cause of" before "nature." More probably "Natur" is a slip for "Ursache," "cause."]

6 It is commonly held that the Christian precept of morality has no advantage in respect of purity over the moral conceptions of the Stoics; the distinction between them is, however, very obvious. The Stoic system made the consciousness of strength of mind the pivot on which all moral dispositions should turn; and although its disciples spoke of duties and even defined them very well, yet they placed the spring and proper determining principle of the will in an elevation of the mind above the lower springs of the senses, which owe their power only to weakness of mind. With them, therefore, virtue was a sort of heroism in the *wise man* who, raising himself above the animal nature of man, is sufficient for himself, and while he prescribes duties to others is himself raised above them, and is not subject to any temptation to transgress the moral law. All this, however, they could not have done if they had conceived this law in all its purity and strictness, as the precept of the Gospel does. When I give the name *idea* to a perfection to which nothing adequate can be given in experience, it does not follow that the moral ideas are something transcendent, that is something of which we could not even determine the concept adequately, or of which it is uncertain whether there is any object corresponding to it at all (270), as is the case with the ideas of speculative reason; on the contrary, being types of practical perfection, they serve as the indispensable rule of conduct and likewise as the *standard of comparison*. Now if I consider *Christian morals* on their philosophical side, then compared with the ideas of the Greek schools they would appear as

follows: the ideas of the *Cynics*, the *Epicureans*, the *Stoics*, and the *Christians* are: *simplicity of nature, prudence, wisdom*, and *holiness*. In respect of the way of attaining them, the Greek schools were distinguished from one another thus, that the Cynics only required *common sense*, the others the path of *science*, but both found the mere *use of natural powers* sufficient for the purpose. Christian morality, because its precept is framed (as a moral precept must be) so pure and unyielding, takes from man all confidence that he can be fully adequate to it, at least in this life, but again sets it up by enabling us to hope that if we act as well as it is in our *power* to do, then what is not in our power will come in to our aid from another source, whether we know how this may be or not. *Aristotle* and *Plato* differed only as to the *origin* of our moral conceptions. [See *Preface*, p. 115, *note*.]

7 [The word 'sanction' is here used in the technical German sense, which is familiar to students of history in connexion with the 'Pragmatic Sanction.']

8 [That the ambiguity of the word *subject* may not mislead the reader, it may be remarked that it is here used in the psychological sense *subjectum legis*, not *subjectus legi*.]

9 [This remark, as well as the following note, applies to the etymological form of the German word, which is God-learned.] Learning is properly only the whole content of the *historical* sciences. Consequently it is only the teacher of revealed theology that can be called a learned theologian [God-learned]. If, however, we choose to call a man learned who is in possession of the rational sciences (mathematics and philosophy), although even this would be contrary to the signification of the word (which always counts as learning only that which must be *'learned'* [taught], and which, therefore, he cannot discover of himself by reason), even in that case the philosopher would make too poor a figure with his knowledge of God as a positive science to let himself be called on that account a *learned man*.

10 But even here we should not be able to allege a requirement *of reason*, if we had not before our eyes a problematical, but yet inevitable, conception of reason, namely, that of an absolutely necessary being. This conception now seeks to be defined, and this, in addition to the tendency to extend itself, is the objective ground of a requirement of speculative reason, namely, to have a more precise definition of the conception of a necessary being which is to serve as the first cause of other beings, so as to make these[11] latter knowable by some means. Without such antecedent necessary problems there are no *requirements*—at least not of *pure reason*—the rest are requirements of *inclination*.

11 I read 'diese' with the ed. of 1791. Rosenkranz and Hartenstein both read 'dieses,' 'this being.'

12 In the *Deutsches Museum*, February, 1787, there is a dissertation by a very subtle and clear-headed man, the late *Wizenmann*, whose early death is to be lamented, in which he disputes the right to argue from a want to the objective reality of its object, and illustrates the point by the example of *a man in love*, who, having fooled himself into an idea of beauty, which is merely a chimera of his own brain,

would fain conclude that such an object really exists somewhere (290). I quite agree with him in this, in all cases where the want is founded on *inclination*, which cannot necessarily postulate the existence of its object even for the man that is affected by it, much less can it contain a demand valid for everyone, and therefore it is merely a *subjective* ground of the wish. But in the present case we have a want of reason springing from an objective determining principle of the will, namely, the moral law, which necessarily binds every rational being, and therefore justifies him in assuming *à priori* in nature the conditions proper for it, and makes the latter inseparable from the complete practical use of reason. It is a duty to realize the *summum bonum* to the utmost of our power, therefore it must be possible, consequently it is unavoidable for every rational being in the world to assume what is necessary for its objective possibility. The assumption is as necessary as the moral law, in connexion with which alone it is valid.

PART SECOND
METHODOLOGY OF PURE PRACTICAL REASON

[1] [Read 'wie' for 'die.']

[2] It is quite proper to extol actions that display a great, unselfish, sympathizing mind or humanity. But in this case we must fix attention not so much on the *elevation of soul*, which is very fleeting and transitory, as on the *subjection of the heart to duty*, from which a more enduring impression may be expected, because this implies principle (whereas the former only implies ebullitions). One need only reflect a little and he will always find a debt that he has by some means incurred towards the human race (even if it were only this, that by the inequality of men in the civil constitution he enjoys advantages on account of which others must be the more in want), which will prevent the thought of *duty* from being repressed by the self-complacent imagination of *merit*.

[3] [*Weisheitslehre*, vernacular German for *Philosophy*. See p. 203.]

INDEX

SUGGESTED READING

ALLISON, HENRY E. *Kant's Transcendental Idealism: An Interpretation and Defense.* New Haven: Yale University Press, 1986.

BARON, MARCIA W. *Kantian Ethics Almost Without Apology.* Ithaca, NY: Cornell University Press, 1999.

BECK, LEWIS WHITE. *A Commentary on Kant's Critique of Pure Reason.* Chicago, IL: University of Chicago Press, 1963.

BENTON, R. J. *Kant's Second Critique and the Problem of Transcendental Arguments.* Denver, CO: Aspen, 1978.

CASSIRER, ERNST. *Kant's Life and Thought.* New Haven: Yale University Press, 1981.

CUMMISKEY, DAVID. *Kantian Consequentialism.* New York: Oxford University Press, 1996.

DEBURGH, WILLIAM G. *From Morality to Religion.* London: MacDonald & Evans, 1938.

FIALA, ANDREW. *The Philosopher's Voice: Philosophy, Politics and Language in the 19th Century.* Albany, NY: State University of New York Press, 2002.

GARDNER, SEBASTIAN. *Routledge Philosophy Guidebook to Kant and the Critique of Pure Reason.* New York: Taylor & Francis, 1999.

GUYER, PAUL, ED. *Cambridge Companion to Kant.* New York: Cambridge University Press, 1992.

HARRIS, GEORGE W. *Agent-Centered Morality.* San Diego, CA: University of California Press, 1999.

HUEMER, MICHAEL. *Skepticism and the Veil of Perception.* Lanham, MD: Rowman & Littlefield, 2001.

KANT, IMMANUEL. *Critique of Judgement*. New York: Macmillan, 1951.

---. *Practical Philosophy*. Eds. Mary J. Gregor and Allen Wood. New York: Cambridge University Press, 1999.

---. *Prolegomena to Any Future Metaphysics*. New York: Macmillan, 1950.

---. *Religion Within the Limits of Reason Alone*. New York: Harper, 1960.

---. *The Metaphysics of Morals*. Trans. Mary J. Gregor. New York: Cambridge University Press, 1996.

KORNER, STEPHAN, ED. *Practical Reason*. New Haven: Yale University Press, 1974.

KUEHN, MANFRED. *Kant: A Biography*. New York: Cambridge University Press, 2002.

O'NEILL, ONORA. *Constructions of Reason: Explorations of Kant's Practical Philosophy*. New York: Cambridge University Press, 1989.

PATON, H. J. *The Categorical Imperative: A Study in Kant's Moral Philosophy*. New York: Harper, 1967.

SCRUTON, ROGER. *Kant: A Very Short Introduction*. New York: Oxford University Press, 2001.

STRATHERN, PAUL. *Kant in 90 Minutes*. Chicago, IL: Ivan R. Dee, 1996.

STRAWSON, PETER F. *The Bounds of Sense*. London: Routledge, 1966.

SULLIVAN, ROGER J. *An Introduction to Kant's Ethics*. New York: Cambridge University Press, 1997.

TEALE, A. E. *Kantian Ethics*. New York: Oxford University Press, 1951.

WIKE, VICTORIA S. *Kant on Happiness in Ethics*. Albany, NY: State University of New York Press, 1994.

WOOD, ALLEN. *Kant's Ethical Thought*. New York: Cambridge University Press, 1999.